MW01074161

WRITING WITH THE MUSE

WRITING WITH THE MUSE

A GUIDE TO CONSCIOUS CREATIVITY

SARA WISEMAN

Copyright © 2014 by Sara Wiseman

Sara Wiseman LLC, 4742 Liberty S #333, Salem OR 97302

All rights reserved. No part of this book may be reproduced or transmitted in any form or by any means, electronic or mechanical, including photocopying, recording or by any information storage and retrieval system, without written permission from the authors, except for the inclusion of brief quotations in a review.

DEDICATION

FOR YOU WHO wait upon the Muse—this book is yours. It is my wish that it will help you to summon the Muse more easily, and that she will arrive not only when you call her, but when you least expect her—and when you need her the most.

Contents

PART 3: THE ALCHEMIST TRANSMUTES

Part 4: Divine Receiving

INTRODUCTION

PERHAPS YOU HAVE heard the myth that creativity is difficult, fickle, fleeting?

That in order to answer the call in your heart, you must give over everything: family, friends, health, security?

That in order to truly create, you must wander in the wilderness, oblivious to all but your book, your art, your vision?

These myths have been swirling around us for a very long time.

For centuries, we've heard tales of the writer in his garret, the starving artist in her studio, the musician who succumbs to addition, the dancer or poet or director or inventor who is forced to endure the greatest hardships in order to produce good work. . . real work.

And yet. . . there is another way to approach creativity.

This new way stems from the understanding that as human beings, we have changed. We have evolved past survival and scarcity and fear to a new way. It's true—we have not evolved

11

completely. But this small shift, this subtle opening and expansion in our collective consciousness is enough to allow us to recognize something very different—that *creativity no longer requires struggle.*

Instead, it is the natural result of experiencing our lives as conscious beings, awake and aware in the world.

In this book, you will learn how to walk in this state of openness, and by doing so, to access unlimited creativity in every moment. This includes the ability to produce good creative work... real work... without the struggle, turmoil and gnashing of teeth we have been led to believe our art requires of us.

It's true, you will be required to surrender. But in laying down your ego, and surrendering to the Divine inspiration that will find you at all times, *you will begin to experience a kind of wild joy, an abandoning to awareness and abundance that you have not known before.*

It is an extraordinary journey to a new state of being.

This book is designed especially for writers—yet it is equally useful for all *conscious creatives*, whether you are an artist, musician, dancer, designer, scientist. It is written for anyone who sees things differently and who seeks to share their unique understanding and viewpoint with others.

Part

1

The Muse Whispers

Chapter

1

Heeding the Call

In every step along the creative path, you will be summoned by a different guide.

The Muse, the Seeker, the Alchemist—each will call, each will invite—and if you answer their intoxicating summons, each will journey with you for a while, taking you by the hand if you need coaxing, leading silently if you need direction, or sometimes simply following, as you walk in the direction of creative awareness.

Each of these callings or trances—Muse, Seeker, Alchemist—will arrive to you in their proper timing, at the proper stage of your journey. They arrive in order, one after the other, as befits the immutable laws of the creative process.

But the first to beckon, the first to seduce?
This is always the Muse.

THE OLD MYTH is not true.

Unlimited creativity is not fickle, fleeting or something to be chased or captured.

You do not need to lay down all that sustains you: the comforts of home, the joy of relationships, the balance of health, in order to attain it.

Instead, unlimited creativity is the *unavoidable consequence of surrender to the Universe* on the spiritual plane; it arrives to us when we gain the true understanding that we are not separate, but One.

What this means is that whenever we enter creative process—whether we're in the first stage of *heeding the call to our work*, or the second stage of *gathering inspiration for our work*, or third stage of *creating the work itself*—all is effortless, abundant, easy.

The three trances

When we work in this new paradigm, we don't work alone. Instead, at each of the three stages of the creative process: *intention, gathering* and *flow* we are supported by the Universe with three callings—three trances, passages, journeys, flows or fugue states in which intention, gathering and flow happen effortlessly, with intensity and humility and joy.

In each of these three trances, fugues or flow states, we go outside ourselves—outside our earth reality to a place that is beyond craft, talent or practice. In this place, we are met by guides, helpers, deities and energies who whisper to us in our mind's eye, our mind's ear; we are led by Universal signs and synchronicities that lead us to our truth; we are provided the knowing to work freely in our process. In these three callings or trances, we are fully supported by forces known and unknown, as the Universe works to create with us, in support of us.

The three trances, fugue or flow states are:

⇒ *The Trance of the Muse*—in which we hear the whisperings of our creative calling.

⇒ *The Trance of the Seeker*—in which we wander the world and are shown what to gather.

⇒ *The Trance of the Alchemist*—in which we enter flow, and transform our creative gathering into its highest possibility.

In this book, you will learn how to enter each of the three trances easily and often. You will meet the helpers and guides who will lead you along each passage of the creative journey, and you will learn how to follow the synchronicities placed in your path, as you seek your art and your craft. Most importantly, you will learn to move outside of yourself, away from ego and attachment, to allow the Universe to move through you in the creation of your art.

Using this approach, you will find that creativity is no longer a burden, a toil, a struggle—but easy, effortless, and the way in which you live your entire life, not just your creative life.

Creativity is spiritual

The premise of this book is that all is One.

This includes writing, all other creative mediums, and the journey of your own life in totality. Thus, art not only imitates life, but vice versus.

When we work in this paradigm, we understand that all creativity is a spiritual act—it is as aligned with Universal laws of intention, asking, receiving, opening, allowing, being, experiencing, synchronicity, message, miracle and revelation as anything else in this Universe.

If you accept this idea of creativity as a spiritual act, of the Universe as One; if you understand the ideas of collective consciousness and collective soul, of our ability to know and understanding anything all the time, and of everything happening all at once, no time or space or matter—then it only makes sense that there is an unlimited, ever-expanding well of creativity to draw from, at all times.

The Universe is infinite; therefore, you always have what you need.

Creative "blocks" as they are called, simply don't exist; they can't. In an infinite Universe, all is possible and available to you—everything you can imagine has the potentiality to be made manifest in your reality.

This also means as you open and surrender to the Universe in order to create your writing or art, you will also enjoy absolute opening of other aspects of your life—such as healing, awareness and enlightenment—areas that you may not have even realized you were working on.

There is no separation

Without exception, all creative exploration affects the creator. There is no vacuum; there is no separation. And while this is freeing, it is also scary—you cannot create in a deep and powerful way, unless you are willing and ready to open that can of worms known as "your stuff", "your baggage," and "your life" and take a look at all the wriggly mess that lies within.

That's where your art is.

I sometimes call this "pulling your heart out of your chest and putting it on the page" for writers. Artists would of course exhibit their hearts on the canvas; musicians into sounds. And so forth.

And in exhibiting your heart, something happens—we become holy in this opening of our inner sacred.

By "sacred" I do not mean that you will be writing holy tracts, or paining pictures of Jesus, Buddha, saints and holy ones, although of course many of you will. I mean instead that you will find and create from your own inner sacred—whatever that means to you. It the deepest, most real place inside of you.

In reaching inside of this hallowed place, in putting your heart on the page, you will of course also create a deep personal resonance in your soul—you will see and understand at levels you might not have imagined, as you open into what the Universe would like you to explore.

It's scary, it's wild, it's beautiful.

There might be no better way to spend your time on this planet.

Showing up to the work

This book contains Exercises to complete in writing or in your medium of choice. Please, don't skip them.

It can be tempting to just "read" them, or "think" about them, and call it day, especially if you are reading on an electronic device. But in this case, because this course teaches a process that uses creative expression as spiritual practice and personal opening, please do the Exercises. Use writing, or your creative medium of choice.

The first reason you'll want to do the Exercises is that they are designed to create experiential learning and to anchor the teachings.

The second is that there is much to be said for simply showing up to the work; the habit of showing up to your creative practice, to sit in the chair, or to enter the studio. If this has sometimes been difficult for you, doing the Exercises will help ease you into the practice.

Of course, if are not a writer, but an artist, musician or other creative being, please adapt the Exercises in this book to your medium. For example, if one of the Exercises is to write from an object's point of view, and you are an artist—please draw, paint or do mixed media for this same Exercise. If you are a musician, then *play* the Exercise with an organic instrument, on a keyboard or on computer—or sing or dance it.

I trust absolutely that you will know what to do.

Keeping a journal

As you work through this book, you'll be asked to keep a journal; in fact, you will be asked to have a journal with you, near you and accessible at all times. This is for everyone: writers, as well as for those working in other creative mediums.

You will be asked to write in your journal. . . or if you want to sketch or diagram or doodle or compose in these pages instead of using words, please feel free.

The main idea is to understand that you will be accessing Universal flow as the source of your creativity, and when this begins to happen, you will soon realize that it is imperative to have a way to record this flow as it arrives to you. Otherwise, it will arrive, and then dissipate—so much floss on the wind.

You may not use this journal every day. But it needs to be kept available, in case you do need to use it. The Muse has a tendency to show up at the most unexpected times and in the most unlikely places. You may receive a poem while walking in the woods, or ideas for your book while in the shower or doing the dishes. You may receive the entire concept for a painting while drinking coffee in a noisy café, or sitting in the rain at your kid's soccer game. You may receive vocal harmonies while grocery shopping. The Muse arrives when the Muse arrives, and her visit is a precious gift not to be wasted. Thus, your journal must be near—at arm's length, available without delay.

In our culture, we have been led to believe that the Muse is fickle, or that she doesn't come often. This belief is not true; the Muse comes all the time. However, if we have no way to record what she is bringing us, her messages are lost.

Again, the Muse is not fickle, but she is subtle. You must be paying attention, open and ready to receive at all times, in order for her to meet you on your path. And when these Divine, beautiful messages arrive, you must be ready to record them in order to take them further.

Working by hand

Please note also that this journal needs to be a regular journal that you write in by hand; not a tablet, phone, laptop or other electronic writing device. You'll need to work by hand to record.

I don't yet understand why this is so, but writing and all creative thought is a different experience when you are writing by hand, then when you are keystroking on an electronic device.

I once had a writing professor explain that *the paper does not know what the pen will write*—that the act of putting pen to paper or paint to canvas or finger to piano key is one of mystery and magic—a merging of soul, mind and body that unlocks a different and more hidden aspect of yourself.

What arrives by hand arrives from a very deep place, and it seems to bring forth ideas and concepts that are both exquisitely vulnerable and true.

When you work by hand as part of your recording practice, you will be able to access this deep and delightful mystery.

Letting it go

Finally, the journaling you'll do as part of this creative process is not something you'll need to save—in fact, it's unlikely that you'll use it again.

While some of you may be in the habit of saving your personal journals and reading them later, this is not that kind of journal. You might think of it as a workbook, a sketchbook, a repository of ideas—it's a place to receive ideas, ponder them and explore further; it's a place to work things out.

In my own creative life, I've made the decision—right or wrong—to be unattached to saving my journals. I carry one with me at all times, and I fill about four journals a month, but I don't keep them—I let them go. In fact, I actually burn them in a ritualistic bonfire once every year or two.

This concept may shock you!

But to my mind, a journal is simply a method of collection—it is not the book, or the poem, or the painting or the song. It's the collection tool—the net—that I catch creative ideas in. In essence, what I receive in my journal is like song heard, or prayer said—nothing more a breath on the wind, noticed and experienced, not needing to be saved.

Creative ideas flit in, are recorded. That's all I needed—a recording point to help me file the ideas in my brain. I don't need the idea on paper, after that. In releasing the need to save or even to refer to past journals, I am able to release what I have already learned, discovered or explored, in order to make way for what is new and to come. Because I trust that there is always more—in an unlimited Universe there is always more!—I don't need to "hold on" to an idea, or worry that my best or greatest idea has already arrived to me and it won't every come again. Instead, I trust that the idea that I need for my creative flow is always arriving to me. What I need always shows up, in perfect timing.

Now, this practice may not be for everyone, but I have found. . . it's enormously freeing to work in this way.

The process of creation—in nature, life and art—is always that of catch and release, create and destroy. *We are always moving to the next moment, the new Now.* There is no reason to get stuck in the past, when the present is so compelling.

CHAPTER

2

THE MUSE WHISPERS

She's come to you already many times. She's arrived as a whisper, a soft voice in your mind's ear. She's arrived as a vision, her hand outstretched, inviting you to follow. She's arrived in your heart, asking that you answer the longing that is deep within. She's arrived so many times offering you gifts, choices—this path, this passage, this journey, that calling.

Always, she asks that you accept each gift with your whole self, in whatever way you are now. She is the Muse; inspiration and discernment, here to help you answer the call that is calling you, the vision that is envisioning you, the longing that has filled your heart to bursting for your entire life.

Allow her now to lead you to your destiny, your life's work, the dream you are dreaming that will become your life, should you choose to follow. Take her hand. Allow her to show you, and to help you choose and discern.

Your way is guided, with the Muse.

I FIRST BEGAN to receive visits from the Muse at the tender age of eight, when my mother gifted me with a diary—a small, red, leather-bound tome with gilded pages and a tiny golden lock. It was meant to keep me busy for the year, but I filled the pages in a month—not with diary entries, but stories, poems, drawings, songs. My mom soon switched me to plain journals: cheaper, and with enough blank pages to keep me busy longer.

From this fortuitous beginning, my experience has been that writing—and any kind of creative output—is never scary, stressful or blocked. Instead, it's a glorious, fantastical adventure in which one can instantly be transported to mystical lands beyond myself.

That's right. *Beyond myself.*

Because the truth is, creativity does not come from me, or my imagination, or from my brain, or from some particular genius that is specifically mine.

In other words, I do not create as I, me, mine. I do not create with force of ego.

To put it even more clearly: it's not about me.

Similarly, it's not about you, and your special gifts and talents and skills. In fact, if we were to be really accurate, we'd understand that creativity really has nothing to do with any sort of genius or special ability in the creator.

Instead, it has everything to do with the creator's ability to pay attention—and then get out of the way and let the creative ideas arrive.

In true creativity, we step aside; we move ourselves aside, and make room for a Source far beyond ego, me, my. We get out of the way—and allow collective consciousness, collective soul to come forth. We record, we collect, we Gather. But none of it stems from us in human form—all arrives from spirit, Universe, Source.

This the only true source for our creativity, and it is a source that is effortless and unending, once you know how the process works.

Unlimited creativity

Before I became an author, I worked for decades as a copywriter and creative director for ad agencies. Let me just say—if you've ever worked on deadline for an ad agency before, you know that "creative block" is simply not an option. When the client is coming in for a meeting, you need to have great concepts, fully illustrated, to show them. If you can't produce—have that creativity come at will, to the beat of a time clock—you won't be able to keep your job.

Back then, on any given day, I might be required to write an ad campaign, direct a photo shoot, write a radio spot or create a video script. Always, the process was the same:

Come to work. Set parameters for the project. Allow an idea to be revealed to me. Jump into creative Flow.

Day in, day out, creativity was unlimited. It was like turning on a faucet and washing the water gush forward. It was effortless. Easy. Even under pressure, I never experienced "creative block".

Why?

Because even back then, I knew one thing: that the source of this creative flow was never, ever myself. Even in the commercial world, where people were running around with titles and deadlines and to-do lists, source was still Source—a big, unlimited Universe of collective information, collective soul, that was always available to me or anyone else, as long as we remembered to tap in, listen and allow it arrive.

As I shifted from advertising to the path of writing and teaching, I spent some time teaching the creative process in workshops and consults. To my amazement, I soon found that many creatives—both novice and professional—were plagued with worry about their work. To my shock, I saw that for many highly creative souls, the river of unlimited creative stream did not always run wet. It often ran dry, so that getting a good idea, or even a mediocre one, was like squeezing a very dry stone.

Why, I wondered, was this so?

I began to explore my own creative process, by now decades old. I looked at what assumptions I held, and what I didn't. What steps I always took, or never did as I scrambled to meet deadlines and complete projects.

And what I found was not only surprising—it was a revelation.

I spent a lot of time considering if what I had learned was true for only me—that it was true of only my particular creative process—or if it was universally true, for everyone—or at least most of us. After trying out the process in workshops and private training, I came away satisfied that this creative process I have come to understand and use will work for nearly everyone. For some, it will be the breakthrough that allows them to produce even more creative stuff, all the time. For others, it will be subtler shift that moves a creative practice to an even higher level.

I'm going to teach you that process here.

Creativity follows Universal laws

Creativity is an energetic process. And just like all energy, it follows a specific order of things, some Universal laws.

When you work with energy using these laws, everything is effortless. But skip these steps, or do them out of order, and everything comes to a miserable, grinding halt.

Now, it's perfectly fine to feel a little squirmy about all this—as a teacher, I often get didactic and march around saying things like "this works, and this doesn't!" So bear with me here. If something doesn't feel right, it's absolutely okay to not agree with what I'm saying; to resist being told "this is so." In fact, I expect that.

People, especially creative people, have their own ideas, and one of the most important things you can do as a conscious creative, is to hold true to your own beliefs and ways of doing things.

I also invite you to recognize that it's still early in the process. Once you see how things work experientially with the three trances, it's going to make a whole lot more sense. My way is just one way, but it has certainly worked for me, and it has worked for many others who now use this process.

So. . . hang in there for a longer, and be open to what happens. Before you know it, you'll have cracked the code of unlimited creative flow for yourself.

The three trances, redux

The source of creative flow is not mine, yours, anyone's. It belongs to the Universe—to a higher energetic vibration that you may call Divine/ One/Infinite/God/All, or any other name you wish. If you don't hold to the idea of Source, you may prefer to use such terms as subconscious, higher self, right brain. If you enjoy assigning personality to your idea of Source, you may call this guides, angels, entities, channeling.

It's all good. And to me, it's all the same.

My belief system is this: all creativity comes from a Universal collective consciousness that we can tap into at any time. Throughout history, this has been named many things, from God to matrix to Akashic records to unified field to Oneness.

The name doesn't matter.

The point is, we ourselves do not create creative thought.

We simply lock into the hum of Universal energy, and receive it.

There are three Trances to this journey:

⇨ *The Trance of the Muse*—in which we hear the whisperings of our creative calling.

⇨ *The Trance of the Seeker*—in which we wander the world and are shown what to gather.

⇨ *The Trance of the Alchemist*—in which we enter flow, and transform our creative gathering into its highest possibility.

We'll discuss these three Trances fully as we move on, for it is here, in these particular fugue states, that we are provided with simple, effortless ways to access flow as we move through the creative process.

You are a receiver

When it comes to creative flow, the part we think is in charge: ego, brain, intellect, talent, self—is most definitely not!

Authentic creativity comes from understanding we are merely receivers for the Universe—we're the conduit, the channel, the tube, the person turning on the faucet, so to speak, standing ready to collect whatever comes out.

In other words, we aren't in charge of what the Universe provides.

In fact, the only thing we can be in charge of is our willingness to receive: to stand at the other end of the tube, the channel, the conduit, and allow what arrives to flow.

Begin to understand this—and we'll delve deeply into this idea so that you'll understand it clearly—and you'll discover how to turn your faucet on more fully, and receive whatever is coming down the "tube" with utmost simplicity and focus.

Begin at the beginning

We've established that you are not the source of your creativity—that you are merely the conduit, tube, receiver, scribe.

In other words: Source is the source!

So, that's the first thing you need to know.

The next thing you need to know is this: creative flow is a process with a predetermined order. And following this order is crucial.

When I started to study the creative process in other people, I found out something shocking: across the board, writers who wanted to write but weren't writing or creative types who weren't producing creative work were all doing the exact same self-sabotaging thing.

They were starting their creative process in the wrong place.

This is like trying to bake a cake without first mixing sugar, butter, flour. Or trying to sail a sailboat without first putting up the sails.

You cannot start at the wrong spot in the creative process, and expect good creative output. In fact, if you do start from the wrong place, you'll end up with something rambling, unfocused and dissipated. . . entirely more trouble than it is worth.

The place to start for creative flow, is always at the beginning.

Exercises

For these Exercises, you will be working with your journal in a diffuse, noticing, non-creating sort of way, simply as a container or opening in which the Muse can reach you. *You won't produce any creative work yet*—instead, you'll simple turn on the faucet of receiving, and the trickle will be slow and gentle at first, without clear direction.

There are three Exercises for this chapter. You may find them thrilling, exciting, invigorating, opening or inspiring, as in "this is great!" Or. . . you may find yourself resistant, you may consider them too simple, you may fight and rail against doing them because you may feel they are too easy. This is also fine.

As we get going, I ask that you simply notice your mind and heart, as you shift and change how you work and how you think about creative work. These Exercises may be different than your own practice, or they may feel like something you've done before that you don't want to return to. Or, they may be new to you. Some parts might fit, some parts might not. I invite you to try them, and to be open, and to see what happens when you allow yourself to do them.

If you have extreme resistance to an Exercise or practice, I invite you especially to look at the resistance, and see what that's about. If you look and find something illuminating there, whether it's anger, discomfort, fear, shame or whatever, that's great. If you look and find that you are "clear" emotionally, and just disinterested in that particular Exercise, respect that.

Allow yourself time and awareness to discern.

In all cases you are the leader and teacher of your own self, far better than anyone else on this planet, including me! Trust that you will know what is best and right for you.

1. Begin a daily journal practice

Write in your journal daily this week, about anything that comes to mind. This can be your personal practice, your way of sorting out what is going on in your emotional world, your daily life. Don't skip a day. Write even when you don't want to or when you have nothing to say. See what happens.

If you already have a journal practice, experiment with what happens when you write at different times of days, in different places, about different things. Try something new, in your practice.

2. Understand yourself as receiver

Write in your journal about the idea of yourself as conduit, scribe, receiver for the Universe. How does this make you feel, to consider the idea that you are not the originator of creative output—you are only the receiver?

For example, you might write: "I'm not the creator, I'm only a tube through which creative ideas flow." Or "I do not create through me, my, I; I create as a receiver of Universal energy." Or, "I receive Universal information, just as all creative beings do. Creativity is a gift for all, not just me." Or, "I'm not in charge of what the Universe sends me to notice, experience or record. I'm just the receiver." And so on.

Write about how this is confusing.
Write about how this is humbling.
Write if this makes you feel angry.
Write about how this is freeing.

3. Do nothing

Do absolutely nothing for 20 minutes each day for the next week. Really and truly do absolutely nothing, and do this by yourself, in privacy.

Turn off all mobile devices, computers, electronica and eliminate all distractions, i.e. other people, kids, animals. Ideally, sitting in nature or in a quiet room is best; but any space will do.

For some of you, it will be very difficult to find this kind of privacy and quiet; you may need to get up 20 minutes early, or go to bed 20 minutes later. Please, try not to carve this time by sitting in your car, as that's not a very lovely environment. I say this because I know from client work that for many of you, that may be the only place you can have privacy. However, seek to find something else, even if the very best you can do is to go to park, or a museum, or an unused conference room, where there aren't any other people.

During this time, allow yourself to get bored, frustrated, freaked out, emotional, lazy, peaceful, sleepy, lonely, unhappy, blissed out, panicked—whatever comes up. Don't read, or look at your phone, or have any other distractions.

Let emotions come up, and notice them. Don't try to fix them or do anything about it.

Just let it happen.

At some point during this conscious silence or stillness each day, close your eyes, breathe deeply, and ask the Muse to send you images or messages that are useful for you to know. Do not worry if they make sense or not.

For example, if the Muse sends you a message of a blue bird, don't worry too much about it—just notice if the idea of "bluebird" or "blue" or "bird" shows up for you in your daily routine this week. Maybe it will; maybe it won't. Turn the idea over in your mind, and allow what comes to come.

Let the ideas received in meditation float through your mind, as you go about your week.

If you fall asleep during this time, respect that you may need more rest than you are getting, and trust that whatever you dream during this time is enlightening and healing you.

Chapter

3

The Muse Invites

The Muse arrives, and presents you with gifts. There are an endless assortment—some big, some small, some sparkly, some plain. They are all containers, meant to hold creative thought. Some will satisfy you for a short while, bringing joy for hours or days. Others are bigger gifts, with more substance, which will fill you up for months, years, even your whole life.

The Muse shows them all to you: the container for the poem, the song, the book, the album, the painting, the exhibition, the dance, the ballet, the song, the opera, the haiku. The single line of superb expression that will captivate you for a year. The single idea that will hold you enthralled for a decade. The container for small and simple pleasure that you may create in your free time. The larger, more expansive containers that are meant for life's work, in which you must fling yourself, body and soul.

The Muse offers you these all—these containers that allow you catch or receive creative expression. Choose just one for now—or go ahead. . . choose more than one. But choose wisely, and choose from your own counsel—not what others tell you or what promises future or glory.

Select instead with your heart, and with your soul.

AFTER WORKING WITH your journal and stillness all of last week, you may find yourself itching to sink your teeth into a writing project; you want to start something, get something going NOW!

However, as now know, there are three Trances to the creative process. I've included them one last time, so you don't have to look them up again:

➤ *The Trance of the Muse*—in which we hear the whisperings of our creative calling.

➤ *The Trance of the Seeker*—in which we wander the world and are shown what to gather.

➤ *The Trance of the Alchemist*—in which we enter flow, and transform our creative gathering into its highest possibility.

If you journey with each of these Trances in their proper order, you will experience a level of inspired, original work and unlimited creative flow that will astound you.

However, if you skip ahead—enter the Trance of the Alchemist say, before you've done the proper Seeking—for example, if you were to start writing a story right NOW, today, without doing any of the wandering and gathering that is required before then. . . well, it's likely that you would end up with a project that somehow doesn't really work, doesn't make sense, isn't what you thought.

It just won't work right, and the more you fuss and fume to fix it, the worse it gets. And then you've wasted a lot of time and energy, and all you've got on your hands is a colossal mess—all because you weren't *starting at the right point in creative process.*

You started at the end, instead of beginning.

It's true: this kind of jumping the gun will produce an initial impetuous creative effort that has a lot of drama and verve—but this flow is not sustainable. If you skip ahead, ignoring the Muse and the Seeker, you'll end up producing creative output that usually doesn't work, is trite and banal, or has a major flaw, or can't be continued, or fizzles out, or doesn't keep your interest and so on.

I know this from painful experience. . . many starts and stops, projects that didn't work out, that had to be abandoned by the roadside. Very discouraging, very wearying, a big waste of time and energy, the very epitome of "learning the hard way."

Again, this is what happens when you don't start at the beginning—when you jump ahead and skip steps, and pretend that you are in charge of your creative output, when really you have nothing to do with it.

The Universe provides all.

When you charge ahead, all ego and drama, what really happens is that you end up back at the beginning, or perhaps even worse—with your confidence shot, and thinking you have some kind of "block."

You don't have a block. You just started in the wrong place.

Creating your container

Many people wander around for years with the belief beating firmly in their chest that "I want to write," or "I want to do art" or "I want to make music."

These are worthy beliefs!

But in order for the Universe to provide the specific creative flow you need, you must first create *a specific container* in which to hold this energy.

This means, you must set intention. For writing, this might mean that you decide that you would like to write something *specific*, such as:

⇒ I will write a one-page poem in the next two weeks.

⇒ I will write a 1,200 word article and send it to so-and-so magazine.

⇒ I will write a 200 page book about this topic.

If you're an artist, it's equally specific, such as:

⇒ I will do a life-size sculpture within four months.

⇒ I will create a three-foot square mixed media piece in three weeks.

⇒ I will create an entire gallery installation at so-and-so gallery by next year.

And so forth, for all other creative forms.

In this first step of creative flow, you *create an energetic container for each project that you might like to do.* This means setting intention in a very specific way:

→ You set the parameters of a project.

→ You set a timeline for the project.

→ You begin to carve out a space and place to work.

→ You arrange your schedule so you've got time to focus on this project.

→ You begin to invite the Universe to send the project to you, as ideas, messages, visions, understandings, synchronicities and so on.

You can create energetic containers for one project, or a whole slew. It all depends on what your interests are, what your goals are, how much time you have, and so forth.

Because I get bored easily, and because my available time falls into both long stretches and quick moments, I personally like to have a lot of containers going at once.

Examples of a big container might be:

→ Writing a book

→ Producing an album

→ Creating a painting series

→ Producing a video

→ Designing a product line

→ Creating a big website

These are big projects which take effort over time—a season, a year, maybe even several years.

When I have a big project going, I also like to have containers open for many smaller projects, such as:

- An article for a magazine

- An ebook

- A series of poems

- Lyrics for songs

- Creating vocal harmonies

- Compiling music for my radio show

- Working with a graphic designer

- Creating an audio product

- Streamlining my website

- Doing art for fun

This way, if I get bored with my big project or I need to rest it for a while, I can turn to the article, the audio course, the design project—and often that shift in focus and energy is just the thing to refresh and revive the bigger project.

In my world, I'm very language oriented—I work a lot in writing, and in audio. I'm also very music oriented—I can't play music, but I can sing and I like to listen to music. I'm not very capable with art, such as drawing, painting etc. When I do projects, I usually work with a designer. However, sometimes, I will do music or art myself—a way of working in a different medium, that opens a new kind of creative aspect.

Sometimes, it's good to mix it up, try something new and just have fun without expectation.

Creating time

For each container, big or small, I'll have a fairly specific idea of when I want to get it done, of the scope of the project, and when I'm going to carve out time to work on it.

For example, when I am working on a book, I have a deadline, I know how many pages the book will be and thus how many pages I need to write per day, and I know that I write best and most focused in the morning, directly after two cups of coffee. I'm pretty much useless as a writer after early afternoon; thus I save that time for doing different sorts of tasks, such as working with clients.

Thus, I set my writing time for morning; this is my highest productivity time. When I'm on deadline, I write almost every day, because that's what my deadline requires. When I'm not on deadline, I work on some of the smaller projects—or maybe I take a break and don't write at all.

Now, many of you won't have outer deadlines yet, and that actually makes it a little harder to know how much time you will need; it also can sometimes make it harder to stay motivated.

Years ago, when I was beginning as a writer, it was hard to stay motivated. I knew full well that my work might never get published—and much of it did not! However, because I was so clear that my calling was to write, I continued.

If you have this calling, you will also have this tenacity, or you will be able to develop this tenacity.

If writing is not your primary calling, the drive will be less.

If you just think you "should" write or that it sounds "fun," you may find that you don't like the life of being a writer after all.

And perhaps you will let go of that dream and allow yourself to move toward what you really do love and enjoy doing.

There is no right or wrong here; we are each unique, and have unique skills and talents. Your desire to write is a personal choice.

There are many reasons for why you write, why you create, and what you're trying to accomplish. Some of you want to be published; for others, getting published is not a pressing concern. These are deeply personal questions, and the answers will also become apparent to you as you work through this book.

Intention as manifesting

Setting intention—creating your container—is the same as manifesting with energy. You determine what it is that you want to create—and then by setting intention, by creating the container, you allow the Universe to bring this to you.

Specifics are important, they are what creates the container. Without the container, there is nothing to hold the creative energy. It's just amorphous, floating around in a Universe as infinite possibility. *You have to create the container, in order for the energy to have someplace to go.*

It's great to have infinite possibility to write a book—some people hold the idea of writing a book their whole lives. But if you really want to write a book, you'll first need to create that specific project container, so the Universe knows what you're trying to create.

No container, no project. It's that simple.

For example, in the past, I might have said "I want to write a book," which was far too broad a container. What kind of book? How long? Soft cover or hard or ebook? Fiction or non-fiction? Traditionally published or self-published? The Universe was trying to help me out, but without a few more parameters, it's hard for the Universe to bring forth what I want.

Nowadays, my container for a project is very specific, such as: "I want to write a 120 page ebook on energy healing, I want to self-publish, and I want to be finished with my first draft by this date." I'm very clear, and because of this, the Universe has no trouble helping me create this project.

Or, in the past, I might have said, "I want to write for magazines."

Now, I'll say, "I want to have a 1,200 word article submitted to this particular magazine, by this date."

The more specific I am, the better.

What I have found is that when I create very specific energetic containers, the Universe always fills them. If I am too broad or unclear, the Universe has trouble manifesting, and I will have trouble working on the project.

You already know

But what if I don't know what I want to create? I hear some of you saying.

Ahhh. Here's the thing. . . you actually do.

Every time you've picked up a book, or looked at a painting, or listened to a song and thought "why couldn't I do that?", you are being clued in to what is within your scope to create.

The Universe has already shown you many, many models or templates of what is possible for you to create. It's plunked these models right under your nose, over and over again.

In fact, I would not be surprised at all, if the Universe has not synchronistically put you in the path of a particular book, painting or song *on purpose*, so you might get the idea of creating something in a similar vein, on your own.

Think back, to what creative output you have always loved. A certain kind of book, or article, or poem, or blog. Look at the books on your bookshelf, or what style of writing you are always drawn to. Look at what you enjoy reading, or viewing, or listening to. What if you could turn on the faucet of creative flow, and create this too?

Great news! You can!

Think back also, to the Exercise you did last week, on being a conduit or receiver for the Divine. What did the Universe tell you then?

Exercises

It's important to figure out what you want to write, and why. Sometimes we just say "I want to write," and are frustrated by what comes to the page– it's like saying we want to go on a trip, and then heading aimlessly out the door in any direction—you won't get very far, and it will probably rain.

Clarifying the genre, structure and even how ambitious we are about going public can be life changing for writers. In fact, some writers may discover they are in fact readers, with no desire to write whatsoever. Some may find that "public" or "famous" does not matter to them—they are content to write strictly for pleasure, craft or other reason. Still others will find that they want to be published, and well-compensated, and anything less will not satisfy. Where do you stand?

This particular Exercise may take some time to complete; if you can do it all in one fell swoop, that's best. If you need to break it into a few sections and do a little each day during the week, please do that. Please find a quiet, private spot, and answer the following questions, in writing, in your journal:

1. Body of work

⇒ In all your time as a human being on this planet, what do you wish to accomplish with your writing?

- List the projects you would like to complete in your lifetime, if they are published, if you are recognized, and what timeframe you would like to complete this work. Do this in detail. Think big.

- Of all the projects you want to do, which project would you like to complete first?

- Which of these projects interests you most deeply?

2. Fame and fortune

- Complete this sentence until you are done writing: "If I were a famous writer my life would be. . ."

- Complete this sentence until you are done writing: "If I were NEVER a famous writer, my life would be. . ."

- Complete this sentence until you are done. "The best thing about being a famous writer is. . ."

- Complete this sentence. "If I am never a published writer. . ."

3. Entering the practice

- In an ideal world, how much time would you spend writing per week. On what days? What times?

- In your real world, how much time could you spend writing per week. What days? What times? Where?

- What other activities do you participating in weekly besides your job/and or family care? Please list them all, estimating how much time they take.

➣ How much free time do you need to write?

➣ If someone who knew told you that even if you spent your life writing, you would never be published, would you keep writing?

➣ If you wouldn't keep writing, what would you do instead?

4. Sharing the dream

➣ Who in your immediate circle of family and friends encourages you to write? How do you feel about this?

➣ Who in your immediate circle discourages you from writing or criticizes your writing? How do you feel about this?

➣ Do you come from a line of successful writers, failed writers, people who wanted to write but didn't? Are you carrying the writing torch for any one?

➣ Where you told as a child that you had writing talent? That you didn't?

5. Planning a project

➣ If you were to start and complete your next project, how much time would you need?

➣ What other steps or information do you need to start this project, i.e research, plot, chapter outline, learn how to write dialogue, get better computer, etc.

➣ Where can you learn what you don't know?

6. Interests and passions

- What themes, situations, time periods or human foibles interest you the most?

- If your writing style was a movie, what movie would it be? Why?

- If it was a song? Why?

- A painting? Why?

CHAPTER

4

THE MUSE GUIDES

And then one day, while you are not really paying attention, not really focused, something happens. You are suddenly aware of the presence of the Muse—not as an idea or a thought, but as an energetic presence with you. You become aware that she is with you, and that she is awaiting your answer.

You may feel her presence in the air around you, or see her beckoning from a sun-dappled forest or a crowded café, or you may simply come to the understanding that she is there, and she is waiting, patiently, for you to decide what you will create.

*The Muse stands in front of you and invites you to
choose a container, portal, receptacle. . . a bowl, if you
may. . . in which to receive. She dangles in front of you
many possibilities: poem, novel, song, opera, dance,
ballet, painting, exhibition. . . these are all containers
that you may select, small or large, simple or complex.
The Muse invites you to choose one—or many.*

AFTER DOING THE Exercises last week, you may find yourself
itching to sink your teeth into a writing project; you want to
start now. While this sort of jumping the gun can produce an
initial impetuous creative effort—it's not sustainable. The result
of just jumping into things without any idea of where you're going usually produces creative output that usually doesn't work,
or fizzles out, or doesn't keep your interest.

Instead, we need to work from the beginning, in the Trance
of the Muse.

At this point on our journey, as we walk along the path of
creativity, the Muse join us—and as we become aware of her
presence, she begins to invite, suggest or offer specific containers or projects for us to fill.

The Muse suggests—she puts the idea in our head.

The Muse invites—she helps us to think bigger, and more
courageously.

She shows us various containers, which we are especially
suited to filling.

And then, if we are very wise, we accept her invitation.

Becoming clear

Many people wander around for years with the belief beating firmly in their chest that "I want to write," or "I want to do art" or "I want to make music."

These are worthy beliefs!

But in order for the Universe to provide the specific creative flow you need, you must first create *a specific container* in which to hold this energy.

You did some work on this in the last chapter. Now, you're going to take what you learned, and get very, very clear.

This means, you must make some choices, set some parameters, determine the scope of what you are trying to do—choose a container that will hold what you have in mind. For writing, this might mean that you decide that you would like to write something *specific*, such as:

- ⇒ I will write a one-page poem in the next two weeks.

- ⇒ I will write a 1,200 word article and send it to so-and-so magazine.

- ⇒ I will write a 200 page book about this topic.

- ⇒ If you're an artist, it's equally specific, such as:

    - ⇉ I will do a life-size sculpture within four months

    - ⇉ I will create a 3 foot square mixed media piece in three weeks

    - ⇉ I will create an entire gallery installation at so-and-so gallery by next year.

And so forth, for all other creative forms.

In the Trance of the Muse, we are guided to choose the energetic container for each project that you might like to do. The Muse serves as inspiration—perhaps we believe we can only write a short story, when the Muse suggests we will be very comfortable in the container of writing a novel.

Or perhaps we have the idea that we are meant to write novels—and the Muse will arrive very clearly, offering to us the beautiful container of poetry, the smaller shorter form, as being more suitable.

We choose. . . but the Muse advises.

And then, when we have allowed the Muse to advise us, we next begin to create our container in a very specific way: you set the parameters, you set a timeline, you begin to carve out a space and place to work, and you arrange your schedule so you've got time to focus on this project.

You can create energetic containers for one project, or a whole slew. It all depends on what your interests are, what your goals are, how much time you have, and so forth.

The Muse will let you know which needs to be done first, which needs the most focus, and so on.

As you saw in the last Exercises, there is much to consider.

Some containers are formal; they require lots of room and lots of space and a commitment to showing up to the work daily over time. Other containers are as simple as getting out paints and seeing what happens for the next hour.

The big project

Writing or creating the big container can be complicated.

It's not so much that you don't know what to do—you will, as you feel your way along, page by page.

It's more that it's difficult to stay committed to the work, when you can't yet imagine that you will finish, or that you will "succeed", whatever that means.

Years ago, when I was beginning as a writer, I found it difficult to sustain the motivation to write; not only did I have four children at home at the time, plus a full time job—but I also knew full well that my work might never get published.

And, much of it did not!

It was hard to resist distractions, duties and this thing we call life.

However, because I was so clear that my calling was to write, I continued. I got myself a tiny, cold office in once was the old changing room of a dance studio, and I headed there as often as I was able, and I began my first novel in that cold, drafty and often noisy place. To this day, the novel is still unpublished—frankly, it's not very good! But during that time, as I chose my container (novel), I learned a great detail about writing, and an even great deal about my own calling as a writer.

If you have this calling, you will also have this tenacity to continue in the face of all distractions.

If writing is not your primary calling, the drive will be less.

There is no right or wrong here; we are each unique, and have unique skills and talents. Your desire to write is a personal choice.

There are many reasons for why you write, why you create, and what you're trying to accomplish: if you want to be published, or if getting published is not a pressing concern. These are deeply personal questions, and the answers will also become apparent to you as you continue.

Container as manifesting

Choosing your container is the same as manifesting with energy. You determine what it is that you want to create—and then by creating the container, you allow the Universe to fill it.

With specific parameters, there is no container.

Without the container, there is nothing to hold the creative energy.

For example, in the past, I might have said "I want to write a book," which was far too big and broad a container—it's unlimited! What kind of book? How long? Soft cover or hardback or ebook? Fiction or non-fiction? Traditionally published or self-published? The Universe is eager to help me, but without a few more parameters, it's hard for the Universe to bring forth what I want.

I need to have parameters, and I need to be specific.

Nowadays, my container for a project is extremely specific, such as "I want to write a 80-page ebook on energy healing, I want to self-publish, and I want to be finished with my first draft by this date."

I'm very clear, and because of this, the Universe has no trouble helping me create this project.

How do I know what project I am doing next? How do I know what I'm supposed to be working on? I allow the Muse to show me. . . I will literally go into meditation, allow the Muse to come in to my reality, and watch as she shows or tells me the best possible containers I am to create and work on right now.

She simply arrives, when I am relaxed, present and aware, and when I call and ask her to help.

Or as another example, in the past I might have said, "I want to write for magazines."

Now, I'll say, "I want to have an 1,200 word article submitted to this particular magazine, by this date."

The more specific I am, the better.

What I have found is that when I create very specific energetic containers, the Universe always fills them.

If I am too broad or unclear, the Universe has trouble manifesting, or may even bring me something I don't want.

Guidance for containers

But what if I don't know what I want to create? I hear some of you muttering.

Ahh. Here's the thing. . . you actually do.

Every time you've picked up a book, or looked at a painting, or listened to a song and thought "why couldn't I do that?" you are being clued in to what is within your scope to create.

The Universe—the Muse—has already shown you many, many models or templates of what is possible for you to create.

In fact, I would not be surprised at all, if the Muse has not synchronistically put you in the path of a particular book, painting or song *on purpose*, so you might get the idea of creating something in a similar vein, on your own.

Think back, to what creative output you have always loved. A certain kind of book, or article, or poem, or blog. Look at the books on your book shelf, or what style of writing you are always drawn to. Look at what you enjoy reading, or viewing, or listening to. What if you could turn on the faucet of creative Flow, and create this too?

Think back also, to the meditation you did in the first Exercise, on being a conduit or receiver for the Divine. What did the Muse tell you then?

Exercises

1. Setting containers

Set containers for two projects you will begin during this course. Be specific about their length, content, time frame—as if you were looking at the finished product already completed.

➥ Write all these details down, for the first project.

➥ If you have a second project, set a container for this one two.

Be as specific as you can. Take time with this. This Exercise may take all week to complete. The more details you can provide, the more possible it is for your project to come to fruition.

2. Asking the Muse

In this Exercise, we will ask the Universe to provide you with further information about the Intentions you have created.

➥ Find a quiet space.

➥ Close your eyes, and breathe in through your nose, out through your mouth several times. Do this until you feel your body and brain start to relax.

➥ Now, think about the first project you just created Intention for, and examine it. Allow any and all ideas to float into your mind. Is there fear? Where or who does to it come from? Is there a memory that surrounds this fear; an event that happened when you were young? Is there anger? Sadness? Joy? Strength? What people in your life show up, when you think about this project? What memories? What emotions?

➥ Examine the second project this same way, and allow what comes to you to arrive.

➥ Ask the Universe to show you the project that you are to work on first. It's possible that the Universe may show you something different than what you've set

Intention for. If this happens, move out of the way, and let this information come to you, even if it is not what you expect or think you want.

⇒ Stay in meditation a while longer. Be open to what arrives. If you feel resistance, or if what you are being shown is not what you thought you wanted, relax and allow this new idea to come into your mind.

⇒ When you are ready to finish this meditation, count yourself back from 10 to 1, and come out of trance. Write in your journal about what you've learned.

⇒ Repeat this meditation a few times this week. Don't move forward until you are sure that you understand not what you want to write, but what the Universe, the Muse, calls you to create.

Part

2

The Seeker Wanders

CHAPTER
5
EMPTYING YOUR BOWL

The Muse has asked you to choose your energetic container—your bowl. Now, you hold it in your hand, ready to begin the next phase of your journey.

Soon, you will be wandering as Seeker in the world.

However, there is one thing you must still do. Before your container may be offered to the Universe to be filled, you must first make sure it is empty. Clean, clear, free from all attachments, every last vestige of ego, me, mine.

You must empty your bowl first, before you begin as Seeker.

In this way, there will be room for what is to arrive.

I WROTE, I painted, I composed, I choreographed, I created.

I, me, mine.

All of these, ego words. All of these, words that signify a misunderstanding of how we access creative flow.

Remember, we are not separate from the Universe. Creative flow is not something that we create, from our own minds. Instead, creative flow is what we allow *to move within us.*

In true creative flow, we move the "I, me, mine" of ourselves aside, and simply become the receiver, the tube, the channel, the conduit for what the Universe would like tell us, show us, bring to us, and place into our container or bowl.

In other words, it's not about us—our small view, our separate self.

It's about accessing big view, big self, All/One/Universe/Divine.

It's about letting the Universe pour through us—about letting our hearts expand as big as infinity—and letting this part of self, our self as One, show up to the page, the painting, the song, the dance.

Thus, before we begin the next part of the creative process in which we will gather information and ideas, fill our bowl, so to speak, we must first empty it of all remnants of misunderstanding—of all false beliefs that creative flow belongs to us or comes from us.

The Universe exists as infinite possibility. Everything that will be created by me or you has been created already—we, as conduits or channels, simply call it into reality.

Again, we don't create. We simple receive, from infinite creation.

In true art, real art, you don't stuff your personality, your talent, your ego into the bowl.

You move aside, so your bowl may be filled.

Detaching from outcome

One of the first things we must empty from our bowl is the expectation or longing for outcome. Not all creative work will be recognized by the world, will be lauded or made famous. Not all will find a published; not all will make money.

Many of the world's greatest authors, artists and composers—those who knew how to move aside so the Universe might fill their bowl with extraordinary gifts—went unrecognized during their lifetimes. Some were simply ahead of their time: misunderstood, ignored, rejected, banned.

So it is.

The true artist is not concerned with this. The joy is in the surrender—in allowing what arrives to arrive, and it giving your entire being to making it possible for this to happen. As we move further into this book, from beyond container to the sheer pleasure of the fugue state that is creative flow, this will become clear to you.

Yes, there is joy in being published—in seeing your writing online, or in a magazine, or a book.

But there is more joy in simply writing—the daily or frequent practice of sitting down with paper or pen or laptop, and moving self aside and allowing the Universe to come through.

Yes, there is joy in having your art exhibited.

But there is more joy in the making of the art itself— in the daily or frequent practice of being with paint or whatever medium you use, and moving self aside so that the Universe may come through.

The joy is in the doing.
The joy is in the practice.
The joy is in the trance or fugue state.
The joy is in allowing oneself to *become the very bowl* that is filled.

Exercise

⇒ Write about how you feel when you are writing or doing art or whatever your creative practice is. Write about how your practice—the doing of it—makes you feel.

⇒ If your work has been recognized by the world, write about that. Not what happened, what was produced or achieved—but how you feel about it.

⇒ Where is the deeper satisfaction for you? In the work, or in the recognition?

⇒ If you could have only one: the work without the exposure OR the recognition without the pleasure, which would you choose?

⇒ Check in again. How do you feel with the understanding that you do not create from *I, me, mine*? Can you allow this to be true for you?

⇒ To what levels do you allow yourself to move aside, to become conduit for the Universe? What are you willing to do?

CHAPTER

6

THE SEEKER WANDERS THE WORLD

*Once your bowl is empty—clean and fresh and ready—
tho Muso will bring you to new teucher. This teucher is
the Seeker; the beggar, sadhu, wanderer in the world. The
Seeker will walk with you on the next path of your journey—that of gathering what the Universe brings to you.*

*The Seeker travels lightly, carrying only a blanket and
a bowl. The Seeker trusts that in the course of his travels,
the Universe will provide for every need. This wandering
and gathering in the mystery is a kind of magic.*

The Seeker does not grasp or worry or fret about what will fill his bowl. Instead, as he walks along in absolute awareness and surrender, all things are attracted as they need to be attracted. Synchronicities and noticings unfold in perfect timing.

The bowl is filled, effortless and easily, by the gifts of the Universe.

As you wander in the world with the Seeker as your guide, you also become the Seeker. Your bowl is also filled.

TO MY MIND, gathering is perhaps the most beautiful part of the creative process. Its stage meant to be lingered in, wallowed in, absolutely enjoyed!

In gathering, you set out as a Seeker with your empty bowl before you and the Universe fills your bowl; it brings you marvelous creative ideas for you to utilize—the same way a lover might surprise you with a blossoming flower, a small note, a thoughtful gift. These discoveries, often showing up in unexpected and synchronistic ways within your day, are the "aha" moments that will fill your heart to bursting with their beauty and depth.

The Seeker wanders the world and receives the gifts of noticing, recalling and remembering. These are gifts of heart's opening, of healing, of experiencing and deep knowing.

Furthermore, when you are in gathering mode, these gifts lurk around every corner, ready to surprise and delight you. Gathering brings a limitless convergence of *synchronicities, signs* and what I call *strands*, yours simply for the asking.

Synchronicities, signs and strands

A few examples of this kind of synchronicity that have recently happened to me:

> *I am thinking about spiritual awakening, about people's experiences with this phenomenon, and I am letting my mind drift as I allow the Universe to bring me more information about spiritual awakening for a book I am working on. One day, I find myself reading a newsletter about a spiritual teacher, and I see the phrase "We will turn your heart inside out."*
>
> *Within less than a minute of reading that phrase, I receive an email from a student, who mentions some teachings she has been following. They sound interesting, so I go take a look. . . there's quite a bit of information. I "randomly" select a page, one page out of probably 100 pages of information, and find myself looking at the words "We will turn you inside out" as relates to spiritual awakening. I know that the Universe, in the span of just a few minutes, has brought me crucial information about the phenomenon, and that I will grow into further understanding soon.*

> *It's a lazy Sunday afternoon on the first day of fall—the Autumnal Equinox—a day when many of my neighbors are inside watching football. It's stormy today, a bluster of wind and rain, and sheets of water pour down from the sky. The trees, still green and leaf laden this time of year, are dripping with wet.*
>
> *Not being a football fan, I decide to sit outside under the covered porch and enjoy the storm. Soon, I am entranced by sound of pelting rain, and the way it splashes down on the green foliage in front of me. In the distance, I watch swirling mist form on the fields below, as the cold rain hits the warmer earth. Overhead, I see*

clouds swirling in a mix of grey and white and black, scudding fast across the sky.

I sink into noticing, and everything seems expanded, brightened, more: the rain, the leaves, the sky, the earth. I become unaware of anything else, and I stay that way a very long time. When I finally "come back" I realize I have been thinking about nothing, and thinking about everything; I feel I have become the rain, or the wind.

I have a dream about being driven in a bright yellow Cadillac; the driver is a large black woman who keeps turning around to smile at me; she is some kind of spiritual guide. In the back seat with me, is another guide. I understand in a flash that even though I often feel lost and that my way is not clear, I am not only accompanied by guides and Universal helpers on the road to my highest self, but I am actually being chauffeured there!

I dream about my paternal grandmother, a woman about who I know very little. The next day, I ask my mother about her, and she pours out information about that side of the family—stuff I've either never heard before, or never stopped to listen to. I think about ancestors and ancestral places, and this informs my thoughts for the next few days. I am overwhelmed by a sense of history, past, past lives and connection.

Gathering in the world

When set forth as Seeker in the world, you're going to need a way to record what you receive in your wanderings. If you wait until after the moment is passed, it will be too late. It's vital to record the noticing as soon after you receive it as possible.

You've already started the practice of carrying a journal with you everywhere—in your purse, backpack, pocket—so that you can grab it wherever you are, whatever you doing, and especially those times when you are walking, doing the dishes, showering, driving, not doing much at all—all those inconvenient times when the Universe likes to show up unannounced!

When you are ready to start gathering, simply head out into the world with your journal and your bowl. The idea is to take your bowl—the energetic container you created with the Muse—and then head out into the world and see what the Universe brings to fill this container.

As Seeker, when you're out gathering in the world, you don't need to do anything. . . your only responsibility is to hold space in a relaxed, non-pressured way. When you're traveling as Seeker, it's good to do normal, everyday things, but to do them in a new state of awareness and noticing: get groceries, get coffee, walk around, do laundry, argue with your sister, take a bath, eat French fries, go to the gym, go to a workshop, buy socks, pick up your child from soccer, take a shower, meditate, dream.

It's also good to do more adventurous things, and apply that same level of awareness and noticing to the new or daring thing: take a road trip, go to a workshop, head into town without a destination, and see where you end up. Go to your high school reunion, a church service, a concert, other places where people gather. Or go someplace totally alone—visit a lovely spot in nature, take a solitary walk, and so on.

It doesn't really matter what you do—outside, inside, busy or quiet.

All that matters is that you're wandering in the world, and like a true Seeker, you have no expectation—you're simply going from town to town holding out your empty bowl, and you trust that it will be filled.

You trust.

That means, you're not trying to figure anything out. You're not trying to solve a creative problem. You're not actively seeking an answer or information. You're not trying to create by force—from the source of me, my, I.

That's not your job, as Seeker. Instead, all you need to do is relax, hold out your energetic container, and trust.

At some point, when you least expect it, the Universe will show up, and you're your bowl with things that you could never imagined on your own. Be ready! Be aware! Pay attention! The Universe will bring you small, sweet and seemingly unconnected snippets, as a gift.

Gifts of noticing

For example, if my energetic container a.k.a. bowl for a project is "write a weekly blog," I might be wandering out and about in the world going about my business, without trying to force a solution—and the Universe might fill my bowl with such moments of reality and insight as:

➤ *One car, rear-ending another, in the Safeway parking lot.*

➤ *A woman slapping her child in a Wal-Mart.*

➤ *A new flower, along the side the road.*

➤ *The way lichen hangs from trees.*

➤ *A guy shuffling out of DMV, his saggy jeans barely covering his butt, his arms scrawled with tattoos.*

➤ *A conversation overheard, at a doctor's office.*

➤ *The sound of a train passing, and airplane streaming overhead, simultaneously.*

⇒ *The cool smell of the morning soil, as I take my dog for a walk.*

All of this, wonderful fodder for a blog!

While I am in Seeker mode, my job as a writer, artist or other conscious creative is not to worry about finding these images or trying to create them on my own. It's not about me, my, I. Ego or cleverness plays no part.

Instead, I simply wander the world, holding out my bowl, and allow the Universe to bring whatever is to be brought to me—or often, me to it. I'm not in change of what I am presented with. I'm not responsible for what I receive. My job is only to be present, and to notice what arrives.

And then, of course, to record it.

Unlimited creative flow

After a while, wandering as Seeker gets really easy.

Effortless, really. Much, much easier than the old method of trying to squeeze creative juice out of a stone.

Not to mix in yet another metaphor, but it gets to be like catching fish when the fish are running. You put your pole in the water and there's a fish, and there's another, and there's another!

It's unlimited abundance.

It's unlimited creative flow.

You don't create it; you just ask for it and receive it.

However, if you're *not* out there Seeking—if you're not out there in your rubber waders with pole in hand actively fishing. . . if instead you're sitting on the beach merely thinking about fishing. . . well then, those fish will not be caught. They will simply flounder away.

Following strands

Of course, not everything you gather is going to make sense. In fact, because gathering works on a spiritual and energetic level, you're going to receive some weird, incongruous stuff when you first set out as Seeker.

What you receive in your bowl might be interesting—but it might not make any sense, or it might not seem to relate to your project.

If this happens, I suggest you allow yourself to stay with whatever you're noticing, experiencing or being shown. And then, reframe what you are receiving with the concepts of *synchronicities, signs* and *strands*—longer links or segments of synchronicities over time.

For example:

> *You're working on a historical novel set in the 1800s. You're in Seeker mode, out walking in the neighborhood, when suddenly you find that where you might normally turn left on your walk, you feel guided to turning right.*
>
> *You can't say how you feel guided, you just sort of know.*
>
> *So, you turn right, and in a few blocks, you come across a tiny record store; it's been there for decades. In the window is a David Bowie poster, during the time he was existing as the Thin White Duke. For some reason, you absolutely stunned by this poster—you can't get enough of it! You whip out your notebook right then and there on the street, and you gather it; you record everything about the poster, the music store, the way David Bowie looked way back then.*
>
> *None of it makes sense—it certainly doesn't have anything to do with your novel—but you don't worry about that right now.*

When you get home, you put on a David Bowie album you haven't listened to in 30 years, and as you are listening, you suddenly solve a key problem of your main character. It just arrives to you, clear and delightful as a bell. The Universe has brought you the solution via David Bowie.

You're working on a romance novel, and you're out into the world as Seeker. You're out driving around and suddenly you notice two people standing together on a bridge. They are either a) lovers professing their undying love or b) preparing to jump together—you get this crazy uneasy feeling that it could go either way.

There's something about the scene that sticks in your head—you don't know why. You pull over the car to a safe place, and you record it in your journal. You gather it, right then and there.

It doesn't make sense that the scene doesn't really fit into your novel, but you decide not to worry about that too much—you acknowledge it was something you noticed, you allow that it doesn't make sense, and you just relax knowing that if you're supposed to understand more, you'll be informed soon. You recorded it in your journal; that's all that matters.

A month later, you're in a place of dire confusion about your characters and their direction, and suddenly the scene on the bridge leaps into your mind. As the memory comes back to you, you soon discover that it solves the biggest, most important climactic scene in your novel. In shock, you realize that a month ago, the Universe brought you this, fully and completely. You just weren't ready to use it yet.

You're an artist working on a gallery exhibit; you've decided how many paintings and what the theme is, and now you're working to produce them. You head out in Seeker mode, not really sure what to do next.

You stop at a café to drink some coffee, and when you get up to the counter to pay you're struck by the way the pastries are set on display in the glass case; something about that causes you to pay attention. You record this in your journal, right there in the café; you even draw a little picture of it.

Several months later, when you are doing the installation for your show, you will suddenly remember the visual elements you see here. But you don't know this yet. Today, all you do is notice how nicely they're displayed.)

And so on.

Ad infinitum.

Effortless and easy.

Again, what you receive while you're out in the world wandering as Seeker doesn't need to make any sense to you at the moment you receive it. It doesn't need to solve any creative problem you're actively working on, either. It may seem disjointed, random, unconnected.

But when you look in your bowl later, you will discover that the Universe has given you exactly what you need.

Thus, when you're gathering, don't have a plan. Head out into the world as Seeker, and welcome what arrives to you. Make room for the odd thing, the chance meeting, the random event, the coincidence, the synchronicity—whatever the Universe wants you to notice. Pay attention to what you're drawn to, what you find interesting, what you see that you normally wouldn't see.

Then record it.

Take a moment, right then and there, and record the David Bowie poster, the lovers on the bridge, or the pastries so neatly and sweetly stacked. Don't worry about understanding it—just record it, right now in your journal or notebook.

Again, don't worry about connecting these snippets, or making sense of them—that part of creative flow comes later. At this point, just receive it, and record it.

The more you wander as Seeker in this way—noticing and then recording—the more easily and frequently the Universe will bring you what you need.

The importance of recording

By now you've noticed that each time the Seeker was given a gift from the Universe, he or she recorded what they received.

They didn't wait.

They whipped out their trusty journal, and recorded the information, incident or emotion right there on the spot.

In some cases, they had to do things like pull over the car, or stand there on the street scribbling in their notebooks. . . you get the idea. Recording is not always convenient, comfortable or what you want to do at the time. In fact, *most times you will want to skip the recording phase.* You'll have these ideas such as "I'll remember this later," or "I can think about this when I get home."

Except—it doesn't work that way. You'll forget, or if you do remember, you won't be able to remember with quite the detail, quite the accuracy. Much of what you saw or experienced will be lost, by the time you get home.

These gifts from the Universe are subtle and delicate, and if you don't get them down right then and there, even if it's inconvenient, even if it's awkward, even if you have to stop your expected trajectory from Point A to Point B in order to scribe in your journal. . . well, you're going to miss it. You'll have nothing but ash in your pockets by the time you get home.

Now, I must add here that it is fine to live this way—going from one experience to the next, in full appreciation of the wonders of this life, existing in Nowness without bothering to do things like recording. It's a very conscious way to live, and it will bring you much heart opening and joy. I live this way a lot!

But if as a conscious creative, part of your journey on this planet is to *gather* some of the amazing stuff of life in writing, art, music, dance or whatever your medium—then, recording is not optional.

It's the only way to capture what you need, so that you can use it later.

Recording as anchoring

I must admit, I don't quite understand why recording is so important; it's a question that fascinates me, and one I haven't fully unraveled.

However, I would suggest that it is a similar phenomenon to how a hypnotherapist or NLP practitioner might "anchor" an idea in the mind by touching your arm as he or she repeats a command phrase.

I believe recording an event immediately in writing or drawing acts as a kind of "anchoring" for the brain. It anchors what we are noticing in the moment, and helps us to sort or store the memory more fully, so that when we go back to it later, we are able to access it more easily and clearly.

It transforms amorphous thought and sensation into language and symbol—ways we communicate to ourselves and each other.

This ties back in with the idea that often don't know *what* we will write until our pen meets paper or our fingers press keys—and we are able to see what has been brought forward by our hand.

In other words, the physicality of writing—the act of moving from brain to paper via the body—is a key component to the creative process. This applies to all expressions: the body painting, the body playing music, and so on.

We are not just brains-on-a-stick. Writing does not just come from intellect or language or words. Art does not just come from mind or vision. Same for all creative forms. All creativity involves some kind of physical process—and there is something mysterious that happens within the body that allows the creativity to come forth.

The mind glimpses the idea, but it is ephemeral—it's beyond language or vision, what we process in the mind.

It's the body—the arm or hand or fingers or voice that transmute the ephemeral idea into a form that can be communicated and shared at a human level—by this I mean in language, in image, in sound, in structure etc.

The body allows us to put soul on paper or canvas.

The body allows us to share our soul with others, in a tangible way that all can understand.

Something about the recording process—the physicality of recording with pen to paper—allows us to anchor the ephemeral idea/thought/concept in the body, so that it can be retrieved in fullest form later.

Knowing what to record

There will be times you'll be out Seeking in the world, and what's arriving will be overwhelming!

Over here, you'll notice the artistry of the chocolate swirl the barista has created in your mocha. Outside, you'll see rain sleet down outside, endless and silvery. A few feet away, you'll become aware of a beautiful woman in a bright blue coat checking her phone—and you'll have the flash that she is contacting her beloved.

Life is such a banquet of senses, emotions, knowing, intuition, understanding, vision, message, feeling! When you are out Seeking in the world, it can sometimes be a veritable onslaught of beauty, horror, grace, chaos—all of it. When you are open and aware, there is always so much, coming at you so fully and so fast. This can make it hard to determine what to record.

What's important? What's random? What's a waste of time?

I would suggest that when you are in Seeker mode, you don't even bother to discern.

Just record it all, as it comes in. Whatever feels important or interesting, record it. You may soon find you are spending a huge amount of time recording—and when you are first getting used to wandering as Seeker in the world, this is just fine.

Often the path to becoming a conscious creative is simply learning how to increase your awareness of the *everything of everything*: the words I use to describe the ineffable idea of how complex and simple, how beautiful or ugly or how beautiful in its ugliness a person, place or situation is. How the *all* of the Universe is displayed before you as a movable feast, as Hemingway titled it, so that whatever you see or touch or taste is spectacular, and there is always more. . . always more.

So, record it all. Record anything that strikes you as interesting as you are roaming around in your life as spiritual sadhu, with your creative begging bowl held out to be filled. Be open to everything. Record what touches you, moves you, captures you, entrances you.

You'll sort it all out later.

How often should you gather?

When you are walking the path of the Seeker, there is no time that you are not holding out your bowl. Every minute of every day, you must be in full surrender to what the Universe might offer you. There is no moment you are not in this place. Even when you forget you are seeking, you still are.

This means:

➻ *Waking up at dawn hearing a blue jay screech is gathering.* Grab your journal from the bedside table, rub the sleep out of your eyes and record.

➻ *Noticing your boss take a phone call in a meeting, and how sad she looks is gathering.* Record it on your memo pad, if you can't bring your journal into the meeting.

➻ *Watching someone roof a house is gathering.* Pull over in your car and write it down.

➻ *Being stuck in traffic and noticing the trash littered on the highway is gathering.* Write it down only if you can do so safely! Record as soon as you are able.

➻ *Watching how the grease congeals on stacked plates in a lunch spot is gathering.* Slip notebook out of purse, observe congealing, record.

➻ *Watching your child perform as a tree in a kindergarten play is gathering.* Enjoy every moment. . . hold it in your heart. . . record it later.

➻ *Making love to your partner is gathering.* Record it in your body, hold it in your soul. . . write it down later.

When your bowl overflows

Now and then, the Universe delivers something really, really big to you, maybe even too big—and it can feel like trying to land a 100-pound fish with a 20-pound line. If this happens to you, the only thing to do is to sit there and record until you have nothing left to tell.

For example, the lyrics and melody lines to our third album, *Songs for Loving & Dying*, arrived to me during a two-week stint of driving my daughter to and from summer camp, about 30 miles each way. I wasn't planning on Seeking while I was driving. It just sort of happened. . . every time I got in the car and started driving those Oregon country roads, the Universe sent a new song.

On the first day the lyrics arrived, I found myself unprepared, and I lost several songs forever. The next day I brought my digital tape recorder along for the trip, and sang into it as I drove. My daughter, who is entirely used to me talking and singing to myself in the car, did not blink an eye!

If I hadn't brought the recorder, I wouldn't have gotten those lyrics. And, quite possibly, those songs on that album might never have come into existence.

It is extremely likely that this be happening to you; in fact, I would guess that it's probably impossible for this not to happen if you are out there wandering in the world, bowl in hand.

The Universe stands ready to bring you full formed, complete ideas, but if you don't catch them when they arrive, they will not reappear in the same fully, fleshed out way again. Ideas are slippery. They are fast. They come quick, and if you do not record them when they come, they will swim away forever.

Be ready.

Exercise

1. Wander as seeker

Wander the world as Seeker this week. Hold your project in the back of your mind, but don't work on it in any practical way. Banish all thoughts such as "I *must* figure out Chapter 15 of my novel today" or "I *must* come up with a brilliant solution for my painting," or whatever it is you might normally think.

Just take your empty bowl, and head out into the world, and see what the Universe brings to you.

Let yourself wander, roam, relax, open—and *every time you notice something different, intriguing or unusual, or something that makes you feel,* record it.

By the end of the week, you will have gathered dozens or maybe even hundreds of times, and you will begin to see how subtly, beautifully and completely the Universe is providing you with creative input.

Resist, in entirety, the urge to *do* anything with this information. It's important to exist only as the Seeker—the wanderer holding out his begging bowl—right now. The Universe is bringing you information, and you are showing up to record it. That's all you need to do for now.

Don't go any further, even if you're tempted to do so.

Keep to the act of recording.

2. Notice synchronicities

After you've walked as the Seeker a few times, take a moment and notice what synchronicities, signs and strands (links or segments of synchronicities) are arriving to you. To do this, answer these questions in your journal:

> ⇒ What situations or parallels or themes are showing up repeatedly in your gathering? Explore what this means to you.

> ⇒ What themes are you working on? What's been on your mind?

> ⇒ What did the Universe bring you that surprised you?

➹ Did you see anything really upsetting? What was it?

➹ Really beautiful? Describe it.

➹ Did you have to go to a new location to see amazing things or do you see them close to home?

➹ How many times a day did you head out into the world as Seeker?

➹ Did you remember to empty your bowl, first?

➹ How many times did you see amazing things and weren't able to record them, i.e.: *A black crow on a pale gold haystack. A deer crossing the road. A red-faced woman drinking a Big Gulp on a very hot day. A young teen girl smoking on a curb.* Let the memories flash in your mind, and try to take them deeper.

➹ What have your emotions been as you've been in the world as Seeker?

➹ What else have you discovered?

3. Try another medium

Gather in a place where creativity is expressed differently. For example, if you are a musician, go to a welding class. If you are writer, take a cooking lesson. If you are an artist, go to a poetry reading.

In other words, see what other conscious creatives are doing. Check out creativity in a different medium, and see how it's different and how it's the same.

For example, I once went to an artist's sitting, and instead of drawing or painting the live model, as all of the other artists in the room did, I *wrote* the live model. It was an extremely interesting experience.

I also sometimes, paint, dance, sing and make things—not because I am especially gifted in these modalities, but because it opens up a new part of myself, and I find that opening in this way unlocks my writing at an even deeper level.

Opening leads to more opening.

As you are watch how other people work, or explore a new medium, notice how the patterns of each creativity process work basically the same way: one layer building up on the next, over the passage of time. One theme expanding and contracting, in a way that stirs the emotions and opens the heart.

If it makes sense to you, write about what you discover.

CHAPTER

7

THE SEEKER WANDERS WITHIN

The Seeker has walked many miles today, connecting with all that is: people, places, conversations, ideas, feelings. The Seeker's bowl has been filled so full! But now it is night: time to shelter, wrap in a blanket, become still.

Within stillness, the Seeker's journey expands a thousand fold. For it is here, in the land of dreams and visions, messages and portents that we receive what we cannot find in the outer world. It is here, where guides, saints and angels tread, that we are given what we most need to know with a clarity and insistence that cannot be mistaken.

In this trance of the mind, the Seeker travels far: through galaxies, dimensions, realms, into the past and the future, into realms that we only know as imaginary, fantastical, Divine.

In the world, The Seeker wanders far. But in the realm of the soul, the Seeker journeys farthest of all.

Even in dreams, the Seeker carries his bowl.

THERE IS ANOTHER method of gathering that does not involve wandering in the world. Instead, it involves traveling inside, within the portals of your mind, of your memory and your ability to have direct connection with all the Divine entities, angels and holy ones here that surround us at all times.

Just as the outside world offers endless abundance, the internal journey is also unlimited. The Universe brings to you unlimited thought, memory, perception, understanding, recall, knowing and idea for whatever creative project you choose to work on.

We can access this information when we enter high-level consciousness states, such as when we are in meditation, prayer, nature, music, dreams. This slowing down, relaxing and allowing ourselves to open into a state of trance and bliss is a way of shifting our awareness and vibration.

In high vibration states, the entire Universe opens to us. We become everything, all at once. This relates not only to us personally—ourselves in the world. It also includes what we need to understand for our creative project.

In wandering on the inside, we are able to receive so much—we are able to contain the entire Universe in our bowl!

Exercises

1. Visualization decks

Get a tarot or archetype deck (I recommend the traditional Thoth tarot deck, or Carolyn Myss's Archetype Cards), and pull out one card at random. Spend some time allowing the different imagery, symbolism, colors, illustrations, and other visual information to inform you about yourself, and what is going on in your life. Record what you discover.

Now, sort the deck, so that you are sorting each card into one of three piles: attracted, repulsed or neutral, as relates to you, and what's going on in your life. Your hopes, dreams, etc. Refrain from using a guidebook to help explain what the card means. Instead, just looking at it, feel your way into it, allow it to bring up whatever it brings up. After you have sorted the cards into three piles, do the sorting again, until you are very clear about how you feel about each card. Write about what you notice about the cards you are attracted to? Repulsed by? Feel neutral about?

Do this Exercise again, but this time, don't do it for yourself, but *for the creative project you are working on.* Allow yourself to be informed by what shows up.

Do this Exercise a few more times during the week, both for yourself and for your project, and notice how the information deepens and changes.

2. Direct connection

In this Exercise, you will simply be, and in this state of being, you will become Seeker within—you will create *direct connection* to the Universe.

To begin, head into nature, or if nature is not available, find a quiet, private place. Close your eyes. Breathe in through the nose, out through the mouth until you feel your body start to shift into relaxation.

Now, allow everything. Don't focus on a mantra, or attempt to release thoughts.

Allow all thoughts, monkey mind and mind chatter. Censor nothing. Allow your mind to roam, race, soar. Allow all emotion. Allow all memory. Allow all verbalizations or sensations to come up in the body.

Allow it all.

At some point, the chaos will begin to build, and to crescendo, and you will feel you are entering the eye of a storm. Allow everything to arrive all at once, full chaos. . . until it reaches a crescendo.

If you are suffering extremely during this, ask the Divine to help you.

If you are scared or frightened, ask the Divine to help you.

If you are releasing old energies at a rate that is overwhelming, ask the Divine to help you.

After a few moments of this storm, you will suddenly notice that the chaos is gone. It has all fallen away. You don't have to do anything to create this; you won't have to release or let go. You'll just suddenly notice yourself in a different realm.

You may receive visions or messages at this time.

You may experience calm, or peace, or even bliss.

Relax in this space, until you are ready to return to ordinary life. When you are ready, simply call yourself back into reality, perhaps by counting back from 10 to 1.

This practice may be harder than you think. Start with 20 minutes. Go longer. Once you lose track of time, it will be a transformative experience.

Do not record anything.

Simply receive in your soul.

3. Seeking with music

This Exercise is similar to the above, but it can be easier for some people, as the music acts as a guide for your journey.

Find a beautiful ambient or healing music CD that you have not listened to before, or are not very familiar with. It can be soft and serene, or wild and emotional. Right now, I am listening to *Primordial Sonics* by David Vito Gregoli, *What the Winter Said* by Kathryn Kaye, *Shanti Orchestra* by Ricky Kej, and our own *Radhe's Dream* by Martyrs of Sound (find it on my website). Search for music without words, or with words in a different language or mantra, and with a range of musical texture—some slow parts, some fast, some quiet, some powerful.

When you have found what you would like to listen to, make an appointment with yourself to listen—really listen to the music. Preferably with headphones. Find a private spot, and get comfortable—wrap up in a blanket, lie down on the bed, sofa or floor.

Now, close your eyes and take a few deep breaths, in through the nose, out through the mouth. In your mind, ask the Universe to bring you what you need in this journey, for yourself, for your project, or for both. Then simply relax and listen for an hour or so, until the music albums is done.

During this time, you may encounter tremendous resistance to the music, you may be transported to other realms, you may see visions, you may encounter emotional difficulties, you may experience body shivering, shaking or other responses. Music helps us to feel our emotions, to see visions and to receive messages. Music opens us up, and takes us to new places.

Stay with it.

When you are done, try to record what you have seen, understood or learned; in recording with pen to paper, you anchor what you have experienced.

CHAPTER

8

THE SEEKER WANDERS IN THE EVERYDAY

The Seeker has nearly finished his journey. He has wandered in the world, seeing all there is to see. He has wandered in the mysteries of the interior realms as well, receiving what has been brought forward as message, vision, energy.

Now, the Seeker has only one more place in which to gather—in the everyday reality of simply what is. By noticing in this way, all fills the bowl.

IT'S GOOD TO wander as Seeker both in the world, and within the self. Both provide different aspects of what you need when you are working on a creative project. When you wander in the world, you see physical things, places, people and situations; you see events, happenings, actions. When you wander within, you see ephemeral things: the past, the future, memories, dreams. You may also receive visions, messages, guides, angelic beings, the departed and more.

All of this informs your creative work.

Your bowl becomes very full indeed, when you wander in these ways—in outer and inner worlds.

However, there is yet a third way to gather, which is neither outer nor inner. It is by simply becoming present to the objects, things and energies around you, as they present themselves to you.

You've heard of fortune tellers, who can read your fortune from a cup of tea leaves?

That's sort of what we're going to do now.

To experience this kind of Seeking, you won't need to do much. You can do it from an armchair, a sofa, or your favorite seat at the coffee house. The Universe will bring it all to you.

Exercises

1. The secret life of objects

Every object holds its own story. If you hold an object in your hand or simply observe it quietly and with full presence—tea cup, Christmas ornament, stone from the beach—you will begin to hear its story. You will begin to hear or sense the tale of where it has been, and who it has been around before. If you listen closely and simply pay attention, you will be able to hear this story very clearly.

You are familiar with the energetic signature of the objects that surround you in your work space or your home. They're probably there because they make you feel good or comforted. But if you take a close look at some of the things surrounding you, especially things that are older, that you've had a while, or that have belonged to other people, you may find that when you move the object from its regular place on the shelf, table or wherever it usually resides, and bring it near to you and simply connect with this object, you can sense much of its story.

Try this now. Take a few objects, and move them to a new spot, such as on the table or desk beside you. Now, one by one, simply tune into the object, and write its story. You can hold it in your hand, or you can just tune in. Once you have a sense of the object, start talking to it in your mind! Ask it where it was from, who made it, what it has experienced, who has used it, and so on. Sink deeper and deeper into this experience with the object. You will be shocked at the information arriving to you! Write everything that arrives to you, without judgment or blocking.

When you are done with one object, take a cleansing breath, and go to the next. Write what comes up there.

2. Sensing story

In the same way that you can tap into the energy and story of an object, you can also gather the same information simply by reading what people write, or connecting to what they create in art or music. Below, I have included some short ads that came from a free classified ads paper. Here are some samples:

Antique kidney shaped desk with glass top mahogany $150 antique dresser walnut $100 arc welder $100 free sofa and love seat.

I have for sale a Dewalt 4.5 gallon air compressor no air have oil less with the wheels and works great. Please call.

Cemetery lots Restlawn garden of sunset make reasonable offer, china hutch cherry wood glass top for display $500 firm.

Roommate wanted could be couple like mother and child, or older, for interview handicap accessible. I'm older lady prefer working person.

Now, it might seem impossible to tune in to these plainly worded classified ads—there's nothing to go on, nothing that inspires. And yet, if you allow yourself to become very still and very present, simply feel your way into the each ad. . . a story does emerge. A story, an energy, a character, a situation, a time, a place.

Try it now: one after the other, simple tune into each ad. Then write down whatever comes to mind.

Again, it's like reading a fortune from tea leaves.

We think there's nothing to go on, when in fact all we need is right in front of us, if we only choose to connect in and see.

This tuning into presence is yet another way of gathering as Seeker—not by wandering in the world, or in the inner realms, but by simply showing up to the everyday objects and information in front of us. Everything in the Universe contains information. Everything. Tune in, connect, pay attention.

It will all arrive into your bowl.

3. Sensing place

Almost every part of the world has been visited by people—human beings—over the millennium. The energy of these souls never leaves the land, the earth, the surroundings. Sometimes these are people from the past, who may have departed this earth—we can sense or see these people as spirits. Often this spirit communication is very clear, so that we can even see or recognize the person's personality, appearance, story, situation and so on. Our ability to receive in this way is uncanny.

Other times, we don't sense departed people, but rather simply the people who used to be there—living in a house, in an empty room, and so on.

Once you begin to work in this way, you may be surprised by how easy this work is for you.

Go to a place where there is history—an old farmhouse, a historical home, places where people might have lived for a long time, but are now departed from the earth. Go there quietly, close your eyes and breathe, and simply relax. Ask those spirits who would like to arrive to tell you their story, to show up. You may not see or hear them in person, but you may have a sense of them arriving into your imagination and your mind.

After you've had this kind of deep noticing, write in your journal about the spirits who showed up, and what you discovered about them and their lives.

Go to a place in nature, where ancient or native peoples once lived. If there is any landmark, such as a sacred stone or marking go and sit there. Do the same process as above, and allow yourself to go back into time, until you can visualize or imagine the people as they were, in that time. Be in this situation for as long as you are able. When you are done, write about it.

Go to some open houses or home tours in your area. As you are touring the homes of where people either live, or have moved from, allow yourself to tune into who they are, and what they are like. How many are there? Men and women? Children? Are they happy? What do they do? What is their story. Let the objects in the house also inform you, with their energy and vibration. Write about it later.

Brew a pot of tea using loose tea leaves. Pour a steaming cup, and drink it down.

After you have drunk your tea, look at the leaves in the bottom of your cup. Imagine you are a fortune teller—simply allow this understanding to arrive to you. Ask the leaves what they are telling you, about anything you are working on as a creative project, or about anything in your life. Simply descend into the energy of the leaves, their placement, how they are clumped or separated, the emotions that come up, or any deep knowings that suddenly arrive to you. Write about it in your journal.

Write down a question about your creative project—what's the next step, how to solve a problem, etc. Now, look up from your journal and let your eyes scan the room or the space you are in. Let your gaze be soft, diffuse, hazy. Continue scanning with a soft gaze, until something catches your eye. Focus on this object or view. Begin to free write about it, just describing it, noticing it, getting it down. After you have been writing for a moment or so, you will notice that you are writing the answer to your question. Try this a few more times, with new questions. The answers are always available to us; there is no time you do not know.

Part
3

The Alchemist Transmutes

CHAPTER
9

THE ALCHEMIST
TRANSMUTES

The Muse has called, and you have answered her. The Seeker has beckoned, and you have accompanied him in the world, in your mind and in the magic of the everyday. In all of these gatherings, you have filled your bowl.

By now, your container is full to brimming with experiences, emotions, glimpses, knowings—you have all you need. It is time to transform what you have gathered into writing, art, conscious creativity.

For this part of your journey, you will spend time with the Alchemist—the one who transmutes base materials into their Divine essence.

YOU'VE ANSWERED THE call. You've gathered what you need.

Now, at last, you are ready to enter flow.

This is the moment where you turn the faucet on. You're going to empty your bowl with the process of your craft, and to begin the act of creating—writing or painting or working in whatever is your medium.

When you finally turn this Universal faucet on, you might feel a little funny—there's a certain irritation, a certain edginess or itchiness, a particular pent up aspect of yourself that shows up as you start flow for a project.

This is normal.

After all, you've been out gathering, standing agape as the Universe has simply provided all you need, without effort or forcing. It's been pretty easy—all you've had to do is pay attention, and record what the Universe drops into your lap. But now, it's time to get more active—to take this receiving, and birth it into your writing, your art, your music.

Again, this transition point, of moving from Seeker into Alchemist, can be a bit tricky and is often fraught with emotion. There's a certain building of energy, a pent up aspect that signifies this change.

If you've ever given birth, you might recall the period of "transition" in labor—the time in which you move from the first stage (contractions) to the second stage (pushing). Between those two stages, lies a state called transition—and it's not a particularly pleasant state. In fact, it's the most intense part of labor. Moving from Seeker to Alchemist is also a kind of transition—and it may be intense.

In order to manage this edgy, cranky intensity of beginning flow, you might find yourself doing some nesting—you might find yourself clearing your schedule, saying no to social invitations, opting out of activities—anything that helps you get yourself into the chair or studio without distraction.

After you've done this process a few times, you'll begin to recognize this edgy, grumpy, pent up feeling as you move from Seeker to Alchemist. Most importantly, you'll start recognize that *this is what it feels like when you need to create.*

Now, you can distract yourself from this feeling.

You pretend to not recognize it.

You can even deny it.

Or, you can instead recognize it—and then succumb. The sweetness that imbues as you enter this sacred flow is worth any initial discomfort at the beginning.

Divine essence

The Alchemist rules all aspects of creation, from the initial flow of expression to the final editing, tweaking, balancing or feng-shui of your project.

The Alchemist has one purpose only—to transform base materials into Divine essence. To do this, the Alchemist must be an extraordinary artist, with the ability to both withstand the passion of unleashed creative outflow, and to endure the less exciting work of refining and polishing until all elements are perfectly arranged, utilized and transmuted.

The Alchemist's passion is to create Divine essence, which in creative expression means originality, emotion, connection and higher truth. It can also be spiritual, but not necessarily in a way that is religious, or overtly spiritual. Whenever you create with originality, emotion, connection and higher truth, it's Divine essence.

An interesting thing begins to happen when you are producing your work at this level of Divine essence: *you become this essence,* too. And then, as the reader, view or listen experiences the work, *they also become this essence.*

And this is probably the true reason we do art: because it is an amazing experience to create such a portal for the human soul.

For example, I am frequently surprised to receive letters from folks who've read my first book, *Writing the Divine.* Part of this book contains *The 33 Lessons,* which are spiritual teachings I received during meditation; I didn't ask for them, they just showed up and I received them. During time of intensive receiving, I was transformed by the teachings—they changed me.

In turn, readers of *The 33 Lessons* write that they have been shifted or changed in small or big ways, simply by reading these lessons.

When the work is true, it changes the artist, and the audience.

It is no small task to become the Alchemist, and to understand that not only are you transforming base ideas into something more, but to also know that you will become transformed in the process, and your readers, viewers or listeners will also become transformed.

This is big stuff.

And yet the rewards for what happens—for the work you create, for how you are transformed, and for what you are able to offer to the world—are so deeply satisfying to the soul that the only choice is to accept the task.

Entering flow

The Alchemist enters fugue or flow state by creating the time and space for intensive and passionate work. Flow state requires no interruption; it also requires enough time on either end to both *get ready to work*, and to *come back down* from the state of working.

You know how a dog circles and circles on his bed, before finally sinking down in his bed? You'll need to have time to circle your work, to get ready, to become courageous enough to begin; this takes time.

You know how rock stars stay up for all hours after a concert, unable to come down off the buzz? You'll need time to come off the buzz of creativity, to let your mind stop spinning and relax back into your life; this also takes time.

This means, you will need to give yourself at minimum of one hour, in which you settle in, take a deep breath, and then write or create without stopping until you are exhausted of this particular idea, and then let it go and have a cup of tea.

Having several uninterrupted hours is much better.

Having days with nothing else to do but flow, is a miracle.

Whatever you can eek out, take.

The point is to jump into the river of flow, and then not move from your spot, until you're done. If you must move, i.e. to go to the bathroom or get a cup of tea, that's fine. But please stay off the phone, social media, avoid discussions with family members, all other ways that you might distract yourself out of flow.

This includes distractions of the craft. Thus, you will disregard: spelling, punctuation, story line, names, details, anything specific, anything that smacks of "right" or "wrong" or "good" or "bad." You can deal with all that stuff later.

If a thought comes up in the middle of flow such as "did I spell that right?" or "is it which or that?", simply thank your mind for reminding you, and then tell it in no uncertain terms, that you aren't doing that type of work right now.

Tell your mind you'll get to it later.

And then return to the work, and simply flow. Write as fast as you can. Push yourself to release everything, and go further than you think you can. Write as long as you can. . . at the beginning this may be only 15 minutes. Over time your endurance will go up, and you will be able to write multiple hours in a day.

Getting out of the way

In flow, there are no errors, mis-starts or mis-directions. The Alchemist guides you in the state of flow, and if you have done your intention and gathering, and if you are really ready, the Alchemist will actually channel the words, images or sounds to you; you will actually hear and sense this information in your head, a Divine download of cosmic communication just for you, and all you will need to do is capture it on the page, canvas and so on.

If you allow this, if you get out of the way and let the Alchemist do his stuff, creativity is effortless and compelling. If you get scared and twisted and blocked and freaked out and say things like "I don't know what to say" or "I'm not a very good writer" or other such nonsense, you will be unable to hear the Alchemist.

Get out of your own way.

Trust that you have set intention, and that you have gathered.

Give yourself an hour, or longer if you are able, and simply allow flow to happen. Don't judge what comes out on the page. Just let it arrive.

The need for privacy

For decades I wrote advertising copy and magazine articles on a tiny desk crammed in the bedroom or a small space in the spare room upstairs. These makeshift spots worked for that kind of commercial work.

But when I turned 40 and decided to return to writing—my own writing—after a 20-year lapse, I knew I would need something different. I had the feeling that time was running out, that I was at a now-or-never point, and if I didn't start writing seriously now, I never would. There was an urgency to getting down to business after so many years of lull. I felt compelled to focus on my work completely and entirely.

I still feel this way.

I needed a writing space, regardless of the fact that I didn't have any money for one. I was at a loss as to how to make this happen—this was before I understood concepts like asking the Universe to help.

I was wandering around our downtown one day with the vague idea that I would like to get a writing space, and I would like to start writing a novel. As I walked along thinking about this, I took a wrong turn. Instead of ending up at the local bakery which was my destination, I ended up at the ballet center—a place I'd been once or twice before. The door was open, and for some reason, I stepped inside. It felt odd to be entering this place, with the dark hallway, and the sound of music coming from the large dance room. A man was inside, pushing a broom across the wood floor, and when he saw me, he said hello.

I cannot recall exactly what happened next, what was said. But as it turned out, he was in charge of renting out space in this dance center, and it was the first time he'd been there in a month—he'd arrived just a few minutes earlier.

"Would you rent that?" I asked suddenly, pointing to the dressing room, about 10-foot square. I had no idea what I was saying or doing—it just came out.

"Well," he said. "There's an idea."

He rented me the dressing room for one hundred dollars a month, and I brought down my desk and my computer and surfed onto someone else's internet connection, and I was set. I wrote my first novel there, with no heat and very little distraction.

I arrived in the morning and left in the afternoon, and sat there and wrote until it was time to pick up my kids from school. I did my freelance (paying) work outside of this sacred time.

Sometimes, I just sat at the desk and squirmed. Sometimes, I wrote furiously and for hours and later realized it was all garbage. But mostly, the Alchemist showed up in this humble space, and taught me how to write.

My first novel has never been published, and probably won't be—first novels are firsts for a reason. But, writing it in that little dressing room taught me the importance of time, space and privacy during the state of flow, when you are actively creating.

I still feel that urgency; that sense of wanting to create all the projects that the Muse offers me. I love—I crave—the feeling of flow, when you're in the middle of writing, and it comes out right the first time, no need for a lot of changes, *fait accompli*.

It's one of the most satisfying things in life. This entire process—of setting intention, gathering and allowing the Universe to bring it all to you, and just when you can't fit another idea/thought/concept into your bowl, you have the joyful, passionate, extraordinary experience of entering flow, and getting it all down.

Flow is true

The very best writing is riveting, shocking, brings up true, wild and sometimes crazy stuff. For example:

> *I killed my husband, and buried his body under City Hall, because he ran over my schnauzer Mitzie. I loved that dog. You think I have it all, wife of prominent politician with a gorgeous home and 6.7 kids, but actually I have sleep issues, and am addicted to Red Bull.*

Where did THAT come from, anyhow?

I don't know. I just wrote it down. I don't have schnauzer, I've never drunk a Red Bull and I'm pretty sure I haven't buried any bodies. It just came out.

So, considered yourself warned—when you are in flow, you will reach further than you thought. You will go deeper. Working in flow will allow you to access parts of yourself you didn't know existed. You will wade in the muck and mud of not just your subconscious—but the basement of your subconscious!

Flow allows you to understand communicate at a level that you did not know you were capable of.

This means that what arrives in flow may also surprise you. You may find that what you write becomes true later. You become intuitive in the state of flow, so that you write something. . . and you are surprised to notice that this "invention" or "creation" in fact comes true.

For example, in my second novel (which has also been published!) I invented a character named Dr. Steve. The name arrived to me out of thin air—it just sounded good for the character. Shortly after I'd finished the novel, I took it to a new writing group. The idea was each of us would share work, and the others would make constructive criticism.

I was nervous when my turn came up; I passed around copies, and began to read aloud. When I came to the part with the Dr. Steve character, one of the men in the class interrupted.

"Is this some kind of a joke?" he asked.

Well, the Universe seems to have a sense of humor about this kind of thing, because his name actually was Dr. Steve. And now, ten years later, he is my husband.

The thing is. . . I made Dr. Steve up, I invented him. He was created in flow state, and after that. . . he showed up in real life. This kind of stuff happens *all the time* when you are in flow state. You open a kind of Universal portal when you are in flow state, and suddenly you connect with everything, and you not only see the future, you create it.

Such is the intuitive power of flow.

Flow reveals all

Something when you're in flow state, you find yourself knocking on doors you might not want to be knocking on—you may find yourself writing about hidden stuff that you don't want to look at or think about. You'll be happily writing in your little space, oblivious to all but the words arriving onto the page—and suddenly a character will show up who you'd prefer not to meet. Or, a situation will unfold that you'd prefer not to experience.

Yikes.

It can be painful, embarrassing, awkward, difficult to reveal your full stuff—what you really think about, even if it's not pretty—on the page.

I invite you to write it anyway. Or paint it. Or dance it.

What shows up in flow is real. It's the true stuff, the real thing—and positive or negative, it's not for us to decide to censor.

Each of us brings an entirely different set of experiences and understandings to the page. Our unique experience is what flow is designed to reveal—and this unique, authentic stuff—no matter what it is—is what we are meant to allow.

For some, what we create will be light, bright and encouraging to others.

For others, what we create will be mysterious, complicated and call upon the ancient archetypes, myths and legends of the human soul.

For others, what we birth will be painful, raw, shocking and true at the deepest level—it will touch others where they can feel it, and help us to access the human condition.

Allow it all to arrive.

When you are in flow, let it flow.

Return to flow

If you've taken writing courses before or read interviews with successful writers, one of the things that will come up is the idea of butt in chair. This idea of sitting down in your chair, and staying there, until you are done writing 300 words, 1000 words— whatever is your goal for that session.

The idea is that you sit your skinny or well-padded derriere down, and you don't move until you're done.

Hmmmph.

Well.

Okaay.

I gotta admit right here and now that I am not a proponent of this method, because I can't do it myself.

My personality is quite distractable, and for me, what works in not butt in chair, but rather *return to chair*. In other words, I will sit and write, probably for about 15 minutes. After that ridiculously short time, I will need to switch gears, and *I will allow myself to do this*. I will get up for a few minutes, and make myself a cup of tea, or put some laundry in, or take the dog out for a potty break. During this short break of no more than five or ten minutes, I will stay in complete flow, continuing to turn thoughts and ideas over in my head.

Again, *I don't break flow*. I won't let myself get on the phone, or start a new project, or converse with family members, or get involved in something that breaks my train of thought. If the internet is distracting me, I will turn the internet off.

Thus, I do a simple task, and then I return to my chair, still completely in flow, and then I return to writing, and once again I write as long as I can. I can almost always write 15 minutes without a break. Sometimes I can write 30, which would be Herculean! Whenever I get antsy, I allow myself get up for a moment. This breaks all the rules of butt in chair! However, it works for me.

I suggest you find what works for you.

For me, the secret is not in staying in the chair. The secret is continually *returning to the chair*, without breaking your flow state; without allowing other thoughts to intrude.

Now, if you are one of those highly disciplined individuals—and I can think of many of you who have this level of concentration right now—so that you can sit in the chair and stay there for four hours cranking out writing, more power to you. Bravo.

But if you are highly distractible, as I am, this method of getting up, doing one easy thing, and returning the chair, may work for you.

Exercises

1. Entering flow

Find a quiet place where you can work uninterrupted for at least one hour. This means, for one hour you will either work steadily, or you will do as I do—work, break, return to work—without breaking flow.

Turn off your phone, internet, whatever it is that might distract you.

Review your intention; the project that you'd like to work or that you are working on. Hold that intention softly in your mind. If it's a small project, determine if you can finish it today. If it's a big project, determine how much you can accomplish in one hour today.

Now, close your eyes, take a deep breath, and recall all the gathering you've done for this project—everything you've recorded in your journal. You don't need to look at your journal—just allow your mind to think of everything you gathered recently. Simply bring those impressions and visions and ideas into your mind. Don't check your journal to find them; they are waiting in your memory. Access them now, and let them roll around in your mind for a few minutes.

Take another deep breath, and allow yourself to let go of the concept of fear, judgment, failure, success, good, bad, etc. You are just going to fill the page with what needs to come out.

Allow yourself to be entirely free from any concern about typos, spelling or grammatical errors, good writing, bad writing, whatever it is. Take a deep breath, and let all that go. It doesn't matter.

Open your eyes, and begin writing. Continue as long as you are able. When you get stuck, take a mini break. Return. Continue.

Write until your intention is complete, if a short project. Write until you are complete, if it is a longer project.

Do not review, read or even look at your work.

Do not show anyone your work.

Do not discuss it with anyone.

Leave it for the day, and go do something else.

Take your notebook with you, in case the Universe would like to share some new ideas with you.

Repeat this process daily, or as often as you can, this week.

2. Being available to flow

After this first experience of flow, it's important to understand that this experience is not just a one-time thing. It's something that you'll be repeating on a regular basis.

It's a habit—a practice.

That means some of you will be writing several hours a day. Others may be able to write for several hours a week, carving out time by getting up early, during your lunch break, by slipping off to the library or café on the weekends.

The time is there, even for the busiest schedules.

If your schedule is truly too busy for writing, pare it down. Take a look now, at how available you can be to flow:

➥ Review your schedule for the next week. How many sessions of flow can you do per day? Per week?

➥ How long do you need per session? 20 minutes? 40 minutes? Three hours of uninterrupted time? Remember to include "getting ready" and "winding down" as part of your flow time.

➥ Do you have a dedicated space for flow? This could be as simple as a spare table in a quiet space, or a spare room in your home, or by renting a writing space. Do some creative thinking this week, about what spaces might be available to you. Ask the Universe to help.

CHAPTER

10

THE ALCHEMIST BALANCES

The Alchemist has worked in passion and energy, and the work has been melded into a new state of Divine essence. In this final stage of flow, the Alchemist comes back repeatedly to the work.

With each passing or passage of intention, there is purification, clarity, balance, fengshui. This is the final task of the Alchemist—the act of transformation of what is rough and raw, into what is true and clear.

THE CLEAN UP, the tweak, the edit. The fengshui. The final stage of flow.

In which you're done with that heady outpouring of ideas and thoughts—in which you've actually produced a work. A first draft. And now, even though it would be insanely lovely to just leave it here, call it done—there is still more work to do.

This second stage of flow—*fengshui*—in which you transmute your raw creative outpouring into something that actually makes sense to the reader/viewer/listener, can either be a lot of fun or a big pain, depending on what kind of person you are.

Some people like to get in with their editing glasses on and just make each sentence sing. Others of us are already on to the next project—we love the flow state, we can't wait to be in it again; to us, this final tweak is boring.

I suggest you force yourself to be a little of both—the careful editor, and the person who says "enough already, I'm done!" This balance is important, to avoid several common mistakes.

First, there is the danger of overworking your project. It's easy to take perfectly lovely prose in first draft—really presentable stuff—and then edit it to death.

Don't do that.

I can't tell you how many edits to do, but I will say this: at the beginning of my writing career I'd probably go through twelve edits. Now, I'll do two or three. My feeling now is: don't worry something, don't fuss and fiddle with it. . . just let it be. If you are working in the proper format of *intention, gather, flow* your ideas will be coming out clearly and cleanly, so they will arrive to the page fully formed and beautifully arranged.

The creative process of *intention, gather, flow* produces clear work, and eliminates the problem of sloppy, unformed ideas that need a lot of clean up.

On the other hand. . . there is a certain magic to going in with your poet's hat on, and simply taking the time to make each sentence sing. This is about turning writing into music, even though you are still working in language. Cadence, rhythm, word choice, meaning. . . all of these are the poet's tools. It is deep pleasure to work at this level of artistry.

Fengshui is balancing

Personally, I have a love-hate relationship with the fengshui process—the final phase of Alchemy. To me, it's a kind of a letdown: you get through the thrill of the entire creative process—all that decision making of *intention* and then the lovely exploration of *gathering*, and the final amazing abandon of *flow*, and you're so excited by what you've created—and then you have to slog back in and take a look and there they are: typos, misspellings, and sentences that don't make sense and plot problems and. . . you want to feed every last page into the fire.

Hold on.

Breathe.

Allow yourself first to congratulate yourself on getting this far, and then simply relax into knowing that fengshui is simply a part of the creative process.

I like to imagine that a work is like a rough cut gem taken from the earth—it might be covered with mud or clay, it might need to be cracked open to show the inner beauty, it might need to be chiseled or polished.

But the gem is in there, intrinsic.

The final act of balancing what has flowed—of fenghsui—is what brings the true beauty and meaning forward.

Entrancing the reader

To my mind, the best writing also allows your reader to experience a type of internal flow, sometimes called *suspension of disbelief*, which means in essence that the moment you enter into a piece of writing, *you agree to go and live in that world*, without questioning anything. So much so that you become entranced, enchanted... as if under a spell.

Writing that is energetically balanced allows you to enter this entranced state easily. It takes you by the hand, and leads you to a place that is so interesting, so easy to follow, such smooth sailing, that you don't even thing to resist walking along the path with the writer.

In order to create writing that will create this state in your reader, you have to effectively remove all stumbling blocks on the path. That means, you have create writing that is clear, clean and smooth, so that the reader can begin reading, and then continue reading to the end or until a natural stopping point, without ever finding an awkward phrase, a half-baked idea, a glaring spelling error, and so forth—anything that will break the spell or loosen enchantment.

In the ancient practice of fengshui, we arrange objects in a room or building so that energy flows—so there is no obstacle to energetic flow. In fengshui for writing, we make sure the energy is flowing in the same way.

The four stages of fengshui

Fengshui takes places on several levels all at once. Here's the way that I move through a written piece, in order:

⇛ *Basic editing*

⇛ *Editing for meaning*

⇒ *Breathing room or rest*

⇒ *Final tweaks*

If you are working in art, or music or dance, it's all the same process but instead of using a computer for writing, you're using whatever art supplies or design program, or whatever music instrument or technology. Let's take a look and see how this process might work.

1. Basic editing

I start here, because it's the part I like the least. I am a terrible typist, and when I am working on a project, deep in flow, I am often typing so fast that I make errors in every sentence; sometimes in almost every word in a sentence. When flow arrives all I can do is catch it the best I can—with spelling errors and typos arriving pell-mell in the midst of all that receiving. It's part of my process, part of how I work, and I have finally accepted it.

In the first pass of basic editing, I will correct for spelling, punctuation and grammar. I sometimes use spell check and grammar check, but often I don't; my voice is so unique, and the writing structure I use is so much my own, that I find that grammar check wants to correct in a way that doesn't sound like me at all.

I suggest you do the same. Trust your own voice, not what is programmed into a computer tool, or even what your editor tells you. Your voice is unique, different and available only to you. Allow it, open it, let it be heard. If you have a particular way of saying things, allow your voice to say it that way. Language is a living art, and the way we express things is changing all the time.

Now, I'm all for people writing with proper grammar and spelling—Chicago Book of Style is there for reason. But I'm also a proponent of writers using their own unique voice—after all, what's the purpose of writing and expressing ourselves, if you're going to sound like everyone else? If you want to do something new and different—throwing out old conventions in language, grammar, spelling and so forth—well, lots of our best writers have done just that.

For example, J.R.R. Tolkien didn't create the amazing, spellbinding reality of *Lord of the Rings* by naming all his characters Dave, Tom and Bill. Mark Twain broke most of the rules of grammar when he wrote the dialogue for Huck Finn. . . and so on.

The key is: if you're gonna break the rules, do it consistently. Remember, your reader wants to stay entranced, enchanted, under your spell. When you are working to balance your writing, this is the most important thing to remember.

Relaxing into the process

Also, be patient during this part of the process. Settle in, relax—understand you're going to be there a while. For me, my first draft contains so many mistakes, it takes quite a while to do this stage of basic editing. It might take only an hour to receive 10 pages—but then three or four hours to correct it. I wish I could do it faster—but I can't. I wish I could do it easier—but it just takes the time and effort it takes.

So it is.

Allow yourself to see the first, basic editing pass of fengshui as a way of becoming more deeply familiar with what you are writing, by being forced to get in there and interact with every sentence, every word.

At this point, focus on editing only the little stuff, such as spelling, punctuation, grammar. You will most certainly notice other things, but hold off on these changes for now. Wait until you have a technically clean document, before you begin to make bigger structural changes.

A note on longer works: If you are creating a longer work, such as a novel, you will want to "chunk" the work in smaller sections. For me, the length I can deal with is about ten pages; anything longer and I start to get disheartened by the task. Again—instead of fighting my innate distractable personality, I simple recognize it, and adjust my working style so I can take a lot of breaks.

I find that editing ten pages at a time, or a chapter at a time, is a good way of keeping your spirits up while you do this fussy, precision editing.

2. Editing for meaning

Now that you've edited for precision, and have a lovely clean copy to work with, you can begin the much more fun and interesting process of simply reading it again—the second pace of *editing for meaning.*

In this phase of fengshui, you will simply read your work. You can read for pacing, you can read for rhythm, you can read for meaning.

Some writers like to read their work aloud at this point; if that works for you, do it. I don't read aloud, but I do read with expression, in my own mind. Some like to print out a copy—I prefer to read on screen and edit as I go.

On this first pass, my main intention is to *read as if I was a first-time reader* to the work. This means look for places where things don't make sense, where they don't fit, where they seem forced or awkward. If these are small problems, I will fix them right then and there.

If there's a bigger problem, I will note it in some way—either by highlighting, or making a little note in my journal, or just holding that thought in my mind—I don't not have an elaborate system.

If it's a really big problem, I will probably hyperventilate a little bit wishing I did not have a big problem to deal with, and then I will go make a cup of tea, relax and just set that problem aside for later.

I am very much a proponent of the idea of dealing with the easy stuff first, and dealing with the hard stuff later. That's just how my personality works—I need constant encouragement and a sense that all is going well, in order to be able to continue doing the work. For me, the key is to make small progresses, and to not allow myself to get disheartened by the enormity of the task.

Once I have figured out the big problems (idea doesn't makes sense, chapters out of order, section needs to be rewritten,) I will clump them together and plan on tackling them in few sessions devoted to big problems.

If the problems are really big and I can't figure out a solution, *I will stop editing*, allow myself to have whatever kind of emotional release I need—storming about, crying. eating a Poptart—and after that's over, I'll set the work aside for a while.

At this point, I'll go right back into the process of gathering, and allow the Universe to inform me of how I should fix the problem, or what I should do. *I won't go back to the work until I have gathered this information*, and am fully clear of what my next step should be. This might take a day, it might take weeks. I wait for it.

I have learned long ago that forcing my ideas never works.

I always need to wait for the Universe.

3. Breathing room or rest

After I've done basic editing and the editing for meaning, and after I've gone back and fixed the big problems, it's time to allow my work to breathe a little without the interference of my own energy. I will set aside the work for a day, a few days, and do something else.

Sometimes I call this breathing room, or *resting*. Another way of thinking about it is that I detach myself from outcome. I separate myself from the work, which most certainly is not my, me, mine.

It's from the Universe. Thus, I can safely detach myself right now, and *allow the Universe to continue to refine the process*. I can move my energy, and myself out of the way during this resting period, with the trust that this distance will bring clarity.

Again, I don't start this rest period, until I've done the fairly time consuming and to my mind boring process of *basic editing*, and the more fun and interesting process of *editing for meaning*. I don't *rest* a piece until both of those processes are done. What I have found from experience is that if I don't get that far on the editing. I tend to not return to the piece, or I get resistant to returning.

As you can tell, in my own personal writing practice, I battle the continual problems of distractibility—I like to "chunk" my work, and I take many, many small breaks along the way.

That said, I do find that resting a piece is one of the most crucial parts of the creative process. Energetically, it's similar to how taking a trip can change your attitude, give you new things to think about, shift your entire view.

The same happens when we rest a piece. We detach our energy from the work. We go on, and do other things, we forget about what we are working on, we allow the Universe to refresh us.

Then, when we return to the piece, we've got some distance. We're literally not as close to it. We can look at it with fresh eyes. And best of all, we don't take it so personally when we find problems or things we still need to work on.

Because we've detached, we can now accept that it's just part of the process. It's all going to be okay. We're just in the process of fengshui, and just like the other parts of writing: intention, gather, flow, it all takes time. Each phase has its own rhythm and emotional feeling.

Again, the rest phase shouldn't be too long—a day, two days, a weekend. There is value in the time that you are not working on writing; but if you let it go too long, you will soon sink into the delicious slumber that is not writing, and if you stay sleeping there too long, it's hard to restart the creative process again. Instead of having a writing practice, you might find yourself watching reruns of Drop Dead Diva, or going to coffee with a friend, or painting the living room.

These are all great activities, but they're not writing.

If you want to put words on a page, you have to show up to the work.

Multiple containers

So what do you while the project you're working on is resting? What do you work on in the meantime?

Herein lies the value of creating multiple containers.

In my own writing practice, I have several projects going at once, so that when one is resting, I will work on the next. If I am resting a big piece, I will work on something small. If I am resting a small piece, I will take a stab at a section or chunk of a bigger project. I'm always changing things up and keeping things interesting, so that once again, I don't get bored.

And, just to confuse the issue completely and go against everything I've just said, sometimes I will take breaks *where I don't write at all*. For example, I try not to write on weekends; I like to get outside or do other things those days. After I complete a big task, such as a manuscript, I might stop writing for a month, even a few months.

Writing is a key practice of my life, *but it is not my life*.

I didn't have this view years ago, but now I do. To be a writer or any kind of conscious creative is a way of showing up in the world. But the experiences of life—the real juice, the real stuff—are what give us something to write about.

I've found you usually can't get those experiences sitting in front of a computer screen.

Thus, while I do work tenaciously, I also understand the need to simply exist in the world, to relax, to enjoy, to explore, have adventures, and simply live as a being, not just a writer.

4. Final tweak

Once you've been through one cycle of *basic editing, editing for meaning* and *resting* a work, you'll go back in for another pass. . . and another. . . and another. This is a final stage of the creative process that I love: the *final tweak* and polishing so that the flow of words read without block or interruption—the reader sails along smoothly, understanding what you are trying to communicate, without any big bumps or hiccups or head scratching along the way.

At this stage, I pay attention to everything all at once, with the same attention I might need if I was telling a story to a four year old.

When you tell a story to a four year old, everything has to make sense. Everything has to be perfectly paced, and travel smoothly from emotional interest to excitement to relaxation. There can't be any distractions. I don't want them to get bored, confused or overly excited. I want them to enter into my entrancement, and just follow along in complete interest, with complete emotionally involvement, until the story is done.

With final tweaks, you'll smooth and amp up your works simultaneously, so it creates this glorious entrancement for your reader. It shouldn't take much, at this stage. It's a final pass—there's not much left to do.

Stop when you're done

At this point, there can be the danger of overworking your piece. If you find yourself feeling confused, unsatisfied, insecure or can't seem to get something the way you want it, let your work rest again. Sometimes, a piece is perfect as is, and in attempting to "fix" it, we will ruin it. As many a preschool teacher has noted, part of the process is knowing when to take the crayons away.

Sometimes, you also just need to have a work be "good enough" and move on. Sometimes, good enough is the best you do—and it that's fine. As work in your craft, your work will get better and better. But if you are new to your craft, you may not have the skills to create what you're trying to create.

You might learn then in next project, or the next.

This is okay.

Work as hard as you can, as passionately as you can, as carefully as you can—and when you are complete, allow yourself to understand and accept this.

There is always another project, a new way to practice and try again.

At this time, I also like to acknowledge how far the work has come—I recall how unformed the work was when I began, how the Universe came to my assistance at every twist and turn, how tenacious I was, and how now, the piece is orderly, true, well-crafted and as close as I can get it to Divine essence.

It may not be perfect, but it has come as far as I can take it.

I also like to see how I have changed during the process of writing this piece, and to remind myself that future readers may also be shifted or enlightened or absorbed by the work when the read it.

Exercises

1. Project review

Take a moment to reflect on the creative process for the various projects you are working on. Answer the questions below for each.

- Describe the project in one sentence.

- Is this project on a deadline? Are you ahead, on or behind schedule?

- Does this project thrill you, excite you and give you joy?

- Is it challenging, complicated or does it have a big learning curve?

- Have you gathered for this project? What are some of the most important things that showed up?

- Have you created your project in flow? How did that feel?

- Have you reached the fengshui stage?

- What stage are you in: basic editing, editing for meaning, resting or final tweaking?

- If there are big problems in this project, what are they?

- Do you need to stop working to gather and let the Universe advise you on how to fix these problems?

- When you think about this project in general, what emotions come to mind?

➤ What other projects are you working on? How do you feel about them?

➤ What project seems the brightest, most exciting and meaningful right now?

➤ Is there any project that you need to let go?

➤ Any new project you need to start?

Using this creative process will circumvent any problems you've ever had with so called creative blocks, stale ideas, working below your level, becoming bored, getting antsy, not knowing what you want to say, or not showing up to your work.

It is a process that is designed to keep you moving forward in spite of yourself, and all the distractions that might convince you to start in the wrong place, give up early, or become distressed by the sheer amount of attention, work and time that writing takes.

If you follow the process. . . really follow it. . . you will notice a change in your creative output, the quality of your writing or art, the deeper understandings and meanings that are arriving to you, and your ability to communicate these in your work.

Simply allowing yourself to journey in the trances of Muse, Seeker, Alchemist, over and over, simply following this four-step process: intention, gathering, flow, fengshui; will take you there.

Chapter

11

The Muse Whispers, Redux

You've completed your project, and now it is time to celebrate. The Muse, the Seeker, the Alchemist all await your presence now, at the long table under the canopy of trees, where they will toast and celebrate until the wee hours.

There is a place for you also at this table.

Sit with your guides now, and give thanks, and be please with the work you have done, the journeys you have taken, the ways the Universe has guided you, and

the tenacity and craft with which you have you pro-
duce your work.

Celebrate, enjoy, and be pleased. And when you
are done with your celebration, release your work like
a pair of doves into the skies, where the Universe the
send them on new journeys, outside of you.

Release your work fully. For tomorrow, or the day
after, or the day after that, is another day. The Muse al-
ready awaits you again, her hand outstretched, waiting
for the time again you will hear her whisper, and accept
her invitation.

BOOK A TRIP to Paris, uncork a bottle of bubbly, host a party of all your friends, take someone out to dinner or let yourself be taken out. Celebrate your accomplishment in the way that suits you best.

Take as long as you need.

Enjoy it.

It is no small thing to write a book, paint a painting, record a song—it can be a life's dream accomplished! It is an even bigger thing to accomplish this in true creative flow, allowing the Universe to guide you at every step.

Allow yourself to be very, very pleased with yourself, and the work you have created via Universal flow; the Divine essence that you have birthed into the world.

And then, when you are done celebrating, allow yourself the magic of energetically releasing your project. That means, letting it go fully. No more edits, no more fussing, nor more thinking about it. No more holding onto it.

Just letting it go.

Sometimes this can be a hard thing to do—we've invested so much into the creation of the work, we have poured so much energy into the work itself, that when the work is done, we miss it. We miss the inspiration of the Muse, we miss our journey with the Seeker, we are bereft to be separate from the Alchemist and his fire.

It's okay to feel adrift, at a loss, without anchor.

Let go of your work anyway. You can send it up in prayer to the Universe. . . you can do a ritual clearing of your desk. No matter if your work is not yet published or in public eye—the creative process of this project is complete. We must create and destroy, create and destroy, create. . . this is the way of things.

After you have released your work, simply wait. You may wait a day, a week, a year. It's hard to know. But suddenly, when you least expect it, you will spy out of the corner of your eye a bright spark of light and once again, the Muse be waiting for you, beckoning for you to follow, whispering of new Universes.

Part 4

DIVINE RECEIVING

CHAPTER 12

DIVINE RECEIVING

The answer to everything exists already. It is inherent in the fabric of the Universe. Whatever you look at, whatever you examine, whatever you see, hear or experience contains exactly the exact energy, direction, solution or awareness that you need to take your creative project further. There's never a time the answer is not there.

YOU'VE DELVED DEEPLY into your creative process, traveling as Muse, Seeker and Alchemist. You've come to understand that true creative flow does not come from me, my, I, but from the abundance of the Universe itself.

Writing is a spiritual and energetic process. It is not something you do by yourself, from ego. Instead, it is something that you open up into—you open yourself, so that you are able to receive what the Universe would like you most to know, understand, see and feel.

There is one more aspect of creativity that you may wish to explore, which is *spiritual receiving*. This is a way in which you step outside of your own self, and become a channel or conduit for Universal information.

Sometimes this process is called channeling, channeled writing, channeled art. *Receiving* as I prefer to call it, has been a profound experience in my life. In 2008 and again in 2011, I received large amounts of spiritual teachings from guides—etheric beings who not only were palpable presences in the room with me, but who came daily and provided me with teachings and information that I not only did not have access to at the time, but did not have the awareness to understand yet.

In 2008, this channeling resulted in spiritual teachings that were included in my first book *Writing the Divine*. This receiving of about 100 pages took place over about three months' time.

After that first episode of receiving, nothing else happened for a long time—I wanted it to, and was willing to, and tried to make it happen—but the guides didn't show up.

Finally, in 2011, I received another long passage of spiritual teachings, about 120 pages, called *The Four Passages of the Heart*; this is now in my book of the same name.

I don't know if I'll receive again, or if I'm done; that's up to the Universe. But I do know that these experiences of receiving have been profound. They are what opened up my intuitive abilities, and what has allowed me to expand as a person—to grow in consciousness and awareness at a level that wouldn't have happened without this Divine infusion.

I have worked with many people who also have the ability to do this kind of receiving; it is a profound and amazing experience. If you are interested in this form of writing, I suggest you try.

It's not for everyone, but if it is for you, it will probably arrive when you try the Exercise below a few times. The complete details for the process are found in my book *Writing the Divine*; please look there to get full instruction. But for now, I've provided a simple Exercise so that you can get started.

Exercise

1. Divine receiving

- ➤ Settle in a private place where you won't have any interruptions.

- ➤ Breathe deeply, and head into a relaxed state. At first, keep your eyes closed, and as you become more relaxed, either keep them closed or allow them to be open slightly.

- ➤ Keep your eyes either closed or in this soft gaze—you don't really see anything, you just sort of see everything all at once.

- ➤ Ask the Universe to allow you to receive Divine writing, spiritual teaching, channeling.

- ➤ Begin writing whatever arrives to you—if you are writing on laptop, try to type with your eyes closed. If you are writing by hand, open your eyes just enough to keep your hand on the page.

➤ If you are not sure what to write, simply listen inside your mind. You will begin to hear words that may or may not be your own mind talking. Write it down.

➤ Continue in faith, without worrying too much about what shows up, or if anything makes sense.

➤ You may notice the presence of guides and other beings in the room; you may see them in your mind, hear them in your mind, or sense them in the room. They may begin communicating with you telepathically. Write down whatever they tell you.

➤ You may feel a higher self arrive to you—a self that is thinking thoughts that you may not yet know. Write these down.

➤ Continue writing until you cannot sense or receive any more. Don't look at what you've written. Just save it.

➤ Return to this practice every day, for the next week, in full faith that each time you arrive, you will become more open to receiving, or if this practice is easy for you, that you will receive more.

➤ You may choose to ask questions to your guides or higher self in writing—ask about your life, your self, your projects, anything at all. Write down the answers.

➤ Do this as often as you like, in the same way you might meditate or pray.

Again, it's hard to know who will have success with this technique. When I first started teaching channeled writing as an in depth process, I believed that anyone could do this easily. Now, I've found that receiving spiritual teachings in this way comes most easily to people who have a) some intuitive or spiritual practice, and b) who are also writers.

Go gently, trust, and try this practice without ego or attachment. If it is for you, it will happen. If it's not, let go and move onto something else. There are many ways to be in this world, and this particular style of receiving may or may not be right for you.

About the Author

Sara Wiseman is an award-winning author and visionary teacher of spiritual intuition. She has taught tens of thousands of students via her best-selling books and courses. She is the founder of *Intuition University*, writes the *Daily Divine* blog, and hosts the popular podcasts *Ask Sara* and *Spiritual Psychic*. She has released four healing music CDs with her band Martyrs of Sound. Sara lives in Oregon with her family. For FREE resources, visit www.sarawiseman.com

66992854R00078

Made in the USA
Lexington, KY
30 August 2017